D1065648

The Junk Collector

What bothers me most about
the idea of having to die

(sooner or later) is that
the collection of junk I

have made in my head will
presumably be dispersed

not that there isn't more
and better junk in other

heads & always will be but
I have become so fond of

my own head's collection.

—James Laughlin

THE WAY

IT WASN'T

FROM THE FILES OF

JAMES LAUGHLIN

EDITED BY

BARBARA EPLER AND DANIEL JAVITCH

A NEW DIRECTIONS BOOK

Interior and Jacket Design: Rodrigo Corral and Gus Powell

Production: Jennifer Van Dalsen

Editors' note: Drawn from James Laughlin's poems and notes for his autobiography as well as from drafts of essays and speeches, *The Way It Wasn't* also contains many excerpts from carbon copies of his extensive correspondence with Guy Davenport, Robert Fitzgerald, Hugh Kenner, Richard Sieburth, Charles Simic, and Eliot Weinberger. Bits have also have also been taken from letters to C. J. Bangs, Anne Carson, Rick Childs, William Corbett, Barbara Epler, Peggy Fox, Donald Hall, Leila Laughlin Javitch, Douglas Messerli, Griselda Ohannessian, and Dr. Benjamin Wiesel. Other correspondents are noted in the text. Acknowledgments are listed on page 342. All photographs and ephemera are from the Collection of James Laughlin.

Printed in China.

New Directions Books are printed on acid-free paper.

First published by New Directions in a cloth edition
and as New Directions Paperbook 1047 in 2006.

Published simultaneously in Canada by Penquin Books Canada, Ltd.

Library of Congress Cataloging-in-Publication Data

Laughlin, James, 1914-1997

    THE WAY IT WASN'T: from the files of James Laughlin / edited by Barbara Epler and Daniel Javitch.

        p. cm.

     "A New Directions Book."

      ISBN-13: 978-0-8112-1667-8 (alk. paper)

      ISBN-10: 0-8112-1667-5 (alk. paper)

      ISBN-13: 978-0-8112-1676-0 (alk. paper)

      ISBN-10: 0-8112-1676-4 (alk. paper)

1. Laughlin, James, 1914- 2. Poets, American—20th century—Biography. 3. Publishers and publishing—United States Biography. 4. Literature publishing—United States—History—20th century. I. Epler, Barbara, 1961- II. Javitch, Daniel. III. Title.

PS3523.A8245Z46 2006

811'.54—dc22

[B]

                              2006023505

New Directions Books are published for James Laughlin

by New Directions Publishing Corporation

80 Eighth Avenue, New York NY 10011

THE WAY IT WASN'T

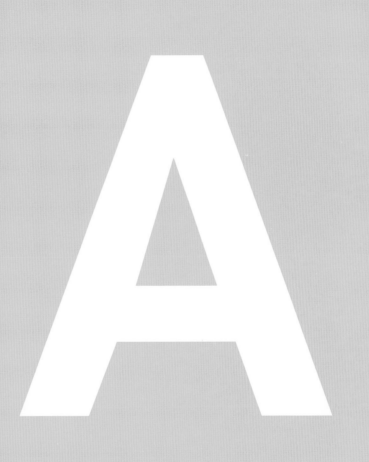

AUTO-BUG-OFFERY

What I'm writing now is my auto-bug-offery. Wild stuff. Mostly fictional. What I wished had happened. "The Way It Wasn't" would be a good title.

AGEE, JAMES

Did I ever tell you about the famous *Advocate* party, when Agee was Pegasus, and we got so plastered we did a Gandhian passive resistance act by lying down in front of the streetcars in Harvard Square? We had about eight of them backed up before they carted us off.

AMERICA

I often feel I'm working in a vacuum, or in a country where few readers hear the sounds.

AUDEN

I first heard of Auden from Eliot. I should explain that in the late Thirties the books of Pound were being published jointly by New Directions and Faber & Faber, where Eliot was an editor. Eliot, known to Pound as the Old Possum, was the only person whom Ezra would trust to edit his work. Hence my visit to 24 Russell Square in London. Eliot asked what I thought of Auden's poetry. I had to admit that I'd never heard of him. "You must remedy that," Eliot said. I did, at once. There was a book-shop nearby in Great Russell Street that had Auden's first book. I took it to a bench in the square . . . and a new world opened for me. As Gertrude Stein used to say—I had worked for her as a typist a few years before—"THE BELL RANG."

I first met Auden himself in Kirchstetten, a little village in the Austrian Tirol, where he and his longtime companion Chester Kallman spent their summers in a small peasant house. I had written ahead to ask if I could stop by for an hour between trains on my way to Vienna. I didn't really expect to hear back from him—of what interest could an unknown publisher be?— but he urged me to come and was most friendly. I found him to be a good talker, very articulate and behind that a vast store of knowledge in many fields. Prosody was one of his specialties. He explained things about the metrics of Thomas Campion and Hopkins, points which were new to me, that no instructor had brought out at Harvard.

Wystan was bilingual in German (plus the Tiroler dialect). He gave me good advice about translators and texts for three of the German-language poets I was thinking of publishing at New Directions: Hoelderlin (who went bonkers), Rilke and Trakl. He and his friend took me to lunch at the Drei Falken, the village pub, where the kaiserschmarrn and the local "rotwien" were excellent. While we were waiting for my train to Vienna to come in he walked me around the village, doing take-offs on local characters in Tiroler, which I could understand pretty well from what I had learned from ski guides in the mountains.

ALTA

Along with Dick Durrance here have taken over the Alta Lodge —just above Salt Lake City. Very beautiful. Like the Alps. Like another world. ND will not cease by any means. This is just something additional, to enlarge life and refresh my soul. Dealing with bookstores not very refreshing to the soul.

So with the money from selling the
Place the brothers bought crockery
And a horse and wagon in Baltimore.
Heading west they sold the stuff
To the farmers in Pennsylvania.
There was enough to start a store
In Pittsburgh. It prospered and then
There was a bank. Then an iron foundry.
God-fearing people, Presbyterians,
Shrewd at deals, saving their money
To make more with it. Their luck was
The Civil War, selling rails
For the Northern armies as they moved
South. In the next generation
They sold pipe for the oil fields
In Texas, structural steel for
Skyscrapers, sheet for Detroit.
Five sons from James alone . . .

Of course I never knew great grandfather, he died in 1882. But I know him from the engraving in the big leather-bound volume, *American Families of Historic Lineage*. (That volume was the racket of a clever New York publisher, "the historic lineators": had to pay to get into it. To have a coat of arms made up and printed in color in the book cost extra.) Our coat of arms has a dog in it, my father always called it "the dog with the sore foot." In the engraving great grandfather has a thin face, whiskers and a sanctimonious, Presbyterian look. He looks kind but they say he was rough with the steel-mill workers (but not as rough as Great Uncle Henry Clay Frick (on my mother's side of the family) who had his works show what for by gunfire in the Great Homestead Strike).

ANGLETON

I never knew that Ellmann was one of the spooks. I knew him pretty well and never suspected. Tangle-on Angleton, as Ezra called him, was a nice person in the old days.

ANDREWS, WAYNE

In 1981 New Directions published Wayne's pungent portrait of Voltaire. It is far from a full biography—only 150 pages—but as the subject himself pointed out, "the surest way of being a bore is to tell everything."

ANN

To reach my study where I write I pass through the dining room where Tchelitchew's portrait of her hangs on the north wall. She must have been about seventeen when it was painted. Her head is slightly turned away from the painter but her gaze is revealed. All of life lies before her. She is looking into her future; a girl whose beauty is in her sensitivity, is looking, with expectation and without fear, into her future.

Why did I have to bring her so much disappointment? Why did I seem to take away part of myself from her? How can I explain it? It was as if something inside me which rightly belonged as well to her as my wife which, for a reason I couldn't understand, I kept trying to keep hidden from her. She never reproached me. She accepted this concealment as a necessity of my nature.

Oh, perhaps we would joke about it. "Poets are a different kind of animal, you know." "You have had a lot of crazies in your family."

AGE

HAIKU

Now when I open my electric
shaver to clean it a fine
gray sand falls in the bowl
at eighty the sands of time.

AUTOBIOGRAPHY

Leily dear

I've decided on the opening epigraph for my auto-bug-offery,
which the Prozac is helping along.

> Daddy, you mustn't be so egocentric. Be eccentric if you want
> to, but there are other people in the world. And it's bad form
> to be a name-dropper.
> L.L.J.

Your loving
Grunpus

P.S. If you'll get Aunt Leila's Korean chest restored I'll pay for it.
Christmas present. Sophie Hawkes might know who can do it well.

AUNT LEILA

Most mornings at Robin Hill when I was living there on the third floor, that was before my first marriage and when the office of New Directions was in her converted stable, she would summon me to her second floor sitting room after breakfast and sit me down by the fireplace for the daily monologue which usually went on for at least an hour, without interruption for I wasn't expected to say anything, just to listen and absorb her wisdom about life, of which there was a large supply. This sounds very boring but it wasn't; it was endlessly fascinating. How had nature or some divine agent packed into this little woman (she was my father's sister) such an intensity of feeling and such a capaciousness of spirit. She would have been in her sixties then and there she sat in her Chinese silk peignoir at the little table by the window that looked out over the gardens (she had attended a horticultural school; in those days young ladies were not sent to college). There, looking out at her beautiful gardens, after she had finished her breakfast, which consisted only of one uncooked egg which she downed in a gulp, there I was, slumped in an easy chair (I was forbidden to smoke in her presence) waiting for the lesson to begin, impatient to have it over so I could get on with my work but curious to know what would come from the lips of the oracle that day. And once she began I was in thrall to her conviction.

She was really old-line. There was a right way and a wrong way to polish brass doorknobs; she told everyone what they should do, and I was the only one who listened . . .

AUNT LEILA

Various of my uncles were pretty crackers. And my dear Aunt, as you'll recall, was, to put it mildly, "difficult"—wrong-headed about certain things. I've decided to put in the facts, but not make a big thing of it. None of them ruined my life in any way. To the contrary, in the case of my aunt, her generosity was what got New Directions started, and her patience with my slew of girlfriends was remarkable, given her background. She disapproved of many things I was doing but she never lowered the boom on me.

She had the ear of an angel, with whom she communicated by automatic writing. She was on the telephone to Mrs. Sage, the medium over in Pleasantville, New York, every day. Curiously, the angel's name was not Lister but Lester. I was often the subject of those letters. She would write, "Dear Lester, I'm worried about James: he keeps making girls fall in love with him."

AIR TRAVEL

The statistical chances of getting blown up are small.

B

BANKS

The other thing I want to urge them to read is *Funny Money* by Mark Singer (Knopf). Have you looked at that? It proves that Ezra was absolutely right about the damage banks can do, here and now. There were these two young men in the Penn Center Bank in Oklahoma City who saw the possibilities of an "ex nihilo" and loaned vast book-entry sums to oil drillers where there waren't no oil, and the moguls of Continental Illinois in Chicago bought the bad loans from them, and there waren't no oil, and the whole scheme went smash and the Feds had to take over Continental to keep the NY banks from going smash by involvement, and so far it has cost the taxpayers about four billion to "preserve the system." Yup, an edifying tale. And I will spare you my account of Mr. Wriston who said "A government can't go bankrupt so loan them all you can," and they did, and the US banks loaned uncountable billions (from Arab petrodollars plus book entry) to Latin America which them spiks have no intention of ever paying back so we may have a real smash-up in a few years' time.

I enclose 2 economics items:
A letter of 1970, found in files, on limitations of Schwungeld.
A story from the **Times** *revealing further nefarious bank shenanigans. Must research this, but assume banks collect interest on these operations.*

BARNARD, MARY

Our first visual inspection of each other was at lunch in New York with Robert Fitzgerald and Florence Codman, the enterprising publisher of Arrow Editions. MB wrote that I was then between recuperations from skiing accidents. She found me "much less serious [than Fitzgerald]. In fact my first impression seems to have been that he didn't have very good sense." She remembers my saying that I loved painting but never went to museums. From which she deduced that there were "Rembrandts and Picassos in his own home." Hardly correct.

The part I liked best in *Assault on Mount Helicon* is MB's account of a few weeks she spent at Norfolk in 1937 doing odd jobs for Jimmy Higgins, who was there running the New Directions office in the stable which my aunt had converted for that purpose. She has caught with gentle wit the character of that bizarre situation—the literary slaves huddled in the caretaker's cottage (Mary was paid thirty-five cents an hour, but she did get free board) while my aunt and her consort exemplified what he liked to call "gracious living" in the great house up the road. I was in Norfolk for only a few days of MB's visit, being enrolled again that year at Harvard. MB reports that Higgins "was bombarded by dozens of instructions that arrived daily from Cambridge."

My aunt, whom Higgins called "the great arranger," took a liking to MB. She thought her most suitable and tried to persuade her to succeed him permanently in the Norfolk post. But MB decided that Norfolk was too isolated and that she didn't have the physical strength to tote heavy book packages to the village post office.

BARNES, DJUNA

Some years ago when she was complaining about her royalties, I volunteered to guarantee her $50 a month against them for life, but she is so suspicious, she thought it was some trick, and turned the offer down.

Speaking of history, Miss Barnes (Djuna, that was) came into the ND office to tell me that the next printing of NIGHTWOOD was to be done on paper that would last for 1000 years. I called the dealers who imported Arches and FABRIANO and sech, but the best they could promise was 700 years. She was very put out with me, declared me an idiot and threatened me with her cane.

FROM DAVENPORT TO JL

I once asked Louis Zukofsky if he ever spoke to Djuna when he met her in his neighborhood. "No," he said, "What do you say to the Minister's Black Veil?"

After an argument with Djuna, who regarded all publishers as her enemy, I protested that I'd always treat her with fairness and the good manners I'd learned at my mother's knee and, at our next encounter, accidentally in the street, Djuna said, "And how's your mother's knee?"

BOYLE, KAY

Memories of a week when I was skiing in Megeve in France. Kay and her then husband, Lawrence Vail, invited me often for meals at their beautiful chalet. It was called "Les Cinque Enfants" – there was a covey of bright and handsome children with names like Sinbad, Apple, and Pegeen, some his, some hers. A happy household.

During the Vietnam War, after she had moved to San Francisco, she picketed the embarkation docks in Oakland where the GIs were shipped off to that glorious conflict. She was arrested, put in prison, and despite her age, set to scrubbing floors on her hands and knees. She was released only when she was found to be seriously ill and sent to the hospital for an operation.

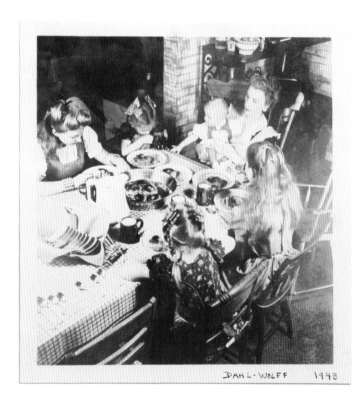

DAHL-WOLFF   1943

BEACH, SYLVIA

Sylvia was a birdlike little figure but she had the strength and energy of a thoroughbred racehorse. She was a chain-smoker and constantly in motion. I remember that quickness of movement as she darted about the shop, the brightness of eye, the sense of humor (she loved puns) and her gift for repartee. Never a dull moment at Shakespeare and Company.

Gertrude Stein was one of the first customers at Shakespeare and Company. She complained that she couldn't find two of her favorite books, *The Girl of the Limberlost* and *The Trail of the Lonesome Pine*, but was placated when she found her own *Tender Buttons* in the shop window. There were expeditions with Sylvia's companion Adrienne to the country in Gertrude's little Ford "Godiva" and many dinners in the rue de Fleurus with American writers who were afraid to approach the awesome Miss Stein on their own. All went well until Sylvia published *Ulysses*. Then a freeze descended and "the flowers of friendship faded friendship faded" to quote the famous Stein poem. I can vouch for this anecdote. I had experience with the literary monolith. The summer that I was working for her at Bilignan, her place in the country, all was going well till she caught me reading Proust. She was deeply offended. "J," she asked, "how can you read such stuff? Don't you know that Proust and Joyce copied their books from my *Making of Americans*?"

BECKETT

I think the only great writer that I really missed out on was Samuel Beckett. I don't know why, but I did. A Harvard class-mate, John Slocum, had told me to look at Beckett, and gave me *Murphy*. I didn't think it was so wonderful at the time. I wish I had.

BERGMAN

Now if you had Bergman's *Three Strange Loves* on your list I could anecdotalize about that. This is an important film because it has my eye in it. Two lovers are arguing in the compartment of a train. Three or four times the camera flashes to a book one of them has been reading which is lying on the seat. What does the camera see? It sees my eye, which is the artwork for the jacket of our edition of Henry Miller's *The Cosmological Eye*. This photo was created by two students in Dunster House, Harvard. They had the negative of the clouds. They made one of my eye and merged the two together. What did Bergman see in my eye? I wrote to ask him, but he didn't answer. If you want to add *Three Strange Loves* to your list you are welcome to this strange little story. Pound used to talk about *le criticisme indirecte,* which he claimed Cocteau practiced.

The Cosmological Eye
by Henry Miller

BISHOP, ELIZABETH

I always wanted to do a book of Elizabeth's poems at New Directions but I managed to muddy the waters for her. I had thought up a stratagem for publishing new poets in group books which I hoped would sell better than the single-poet first volumes which were not doing at all well in those days—if they ever have. The series was called "Five Young American Poets." They were anthologies of five new poets, about 40 pages for each, enough for a good showing of a new talent, and, believe it or not, we were then able to sell these hardbound collections for $2.50!

But Elizabeth wanted a book unto herself. She wouldn't play groupie. Throughout her career, she owed so much to the individualist, cultivating her own plot of ground, not becoming a member of a school. I understand that now. But at the time I was stubborn, stubborn insistent for my publishing project in which she would have been a star. So I lost the chance, I suppose, to be her first and perhaps her regular publisher.

My next effort to "manipulate" Elizabeth—I use the word advisedly, I was always one to try to get my way—was with the Poets of the Month Series. (The Book of the Month people enjoined me to change the name to Poets of the Year; they clamed the phrase "of the month" belonged to them.) I had always loved typography and fine printing. But I didn't have the money to emulate the French *livres d'artiste* or the great English press books. I hit on the idea of a series of 32-page pamphlets of poetry, each one printed by a different fine printer, an artist of design. It seems incredible now but I was able to sell these for fifty cents, or $5.50 for a boxed set to subscribers. The series ran for 42 numbers and attracted a distinguished list: Delmore Schwartz's verse play *Shenandoah*; Rilke's *Book of Hours*; William Carlos Williams' *The Broken Span*; Berryman's first book, *Poems*; Brecht's verse play *The Trial of Lucullus*; Dylan Thomas's *New Poems*; Rimbaud's *Illuminations*; a selection of Hoelderlin; Nabokov's translations of *Three Russian Poets*;

JL AND EB,
ON THE PORCH
OF THE SQUARE
ROOF BROTHEL
IN KEY WEST.

Thomas Merton's first book, *Thirty Poems*; and a selected poems of Melville were a few of the high spots.

I desperately wanted to enlist Elizabeth for the Poets of the Year Series but I failed to persuade her. By that time she had finished enough poems for a much longer book and she wanted the impact of a collection larger than a 32-page pamphlet. We were both politely stubborn. She published *North and South* with Houghton Mifflin and then went on to work with my good friend Bob Giroux. Bob, who is at present editing Elizabeth's letters, is by all odds the greatest literary editor of our time.

In those earlier years I don't think I had actually seen Elizabeth more than once or twice. My chance to get to know her better came in 1940 when Tennessee invited Gertrude and myself down to visit him in Key West. Elizabeth was in Key West that winter with her friend Louise Crane. Tennessee and Elizabeth were congenial. He liked bright girls as long as he didn't have to get involved with them. . . .

We had some very pleasant dinners with Elizabeth and Louise. I found in Elizabeth a delicacy akin to that of her poems, but also a nice sense of humor. I remember quite a twinkle.

Tennessee had walked me around the town a bit. I was struck by an old wooden building that had a square roof. The place was indeed known as "The Square Roof." It was a brothel where the young ladies were of dusky complexion. It turned out that Elizabeth and Louise had researched "The Square Roof" in the line of literary duty. "I have a friend there," she told us, "would you like to meet them here? We could pay a call." Not meaning a professional call but a social one. Elizabeth arranged the invitation to tea. Tennessee suggested we doll up a bit to show we were chums not customers. It was one of the few times I saw him in a necktie. Tenn was small but he could look quite handsome when he took off his "shades;" they were his shield from the world. He was shy but what a smile when he liked someone!

The madam of the "Square Roof" was elderly. She must have been very pretty once. She had somewhat elegant manners. She enjoyed making polite conversation. I wanted to ask her if Hemingway had ever been a patron of the house when he lived in Key West but decided I'd better not. A confidential matter. The young ladies were of various dimensions, including one who was quite rotund. A special taste? They were wearing their "church" dresses—their guardian informed us that some were Methodists and some Baptists and that they attended Sunday services regularly. They were not talkative, though Elizabeth and Louise tried to draw them out, but it was evident from their demeanor that they were glad to see us. The madam poured from an antique tea service into flowered cups which were daintily grasped by the young ladies. Oreo cookies were served, my favorites.

Suddenly one of the girls—a light-skinned charmer—enquired if we would like to see her room. A moment's silence but Elizabeth said that we indeed would. We all traipsed upstairs. I found the girl's room touching and sweet. The bedstead with its high carved back could have come out of any bourgeois house in Bordeaux. A fancy purple silk spread. Lace covers on the pillows. An embroidered flower-print rug on the floor. The mirror on the dresser was nearly as tall as a pierglass. Below it a small glass vase with several stalks of jasmine in it. Standing frames with photographs of a handsome family from old people to children. On a small table by the head of the bed a Gideon bible. But, most moving of all, sitting propped against the bed pillows a row of dolls in dresses that surely the owner had stitched. What we saw there in that room touched us all to silence. We trooped downstairs and thanked them all for our visit. They all seemed so cheerful and happy.

I've often hoped that an account of our visit to the "Square Roof" would turn up in one of Elizabeth's poems, but if she ever wrote it I've never seen it.

BOOKSELLING

And I do not let myself get downhearted. I brood, but when the
time comes to go into the bookstores and fight I fight with all
I've got. Most of the buyers are women—bitches: rather stupid
middle-aged women of no background, worried about business,
positively hating a book that requires intelligence to read and
sell. These creatures I must woo. I must manage somehow to
get through their shell and make them break their own rules,
make them put a good book, a book of poetry, on their shelves.
Selling is really a great art, and I am just a novice at it, but it gets
into your blood. To size up the buyer at a glance, in the half
instant that you have free as you come into the shop, to make
instantly your judgment of the line you will take, and then to
attack . . . and not to give way at the first defeat but keep at it,
trying every last little dodge that you've picked up from past
experience. Anything to leave the books behind you, or rather,
come away with an order. It is like some kind of insect deposit-
ing pollen where it isn't wanted. You believe in the seed you
carry. You feel sure if you can just leave the books in view in the
store someone will come in and buy them. But you have first to
overcome this Cerberus, this unattractive middle-aged woman
with unhappy lines on her face, this symbol of Babbitry and stu-
pidity. She is the enemy, and also the friend. My God how you
love her after she has bought something. All your loathing runs
away and you are friends. You sit there for a moment after the
sale, in a sort of lull after a tempest, and talk a little shop in a
soft, pleasant way, with all the ferocity out of you and a feeling
in you of actual bliss, as though you had just conceived a child.

JL TO
DYLAN THOMAS
4.30.38

BORGESE, ELISABETH MANN

The heat is combusting me. I cannot sleep, work or eat. Gertrude wants to cremate me, but I insist on the worms because my little Schwesterli, Elisabetchen, the daughter of T. Mann, insists that the corpses of poets feel the final flames, this in her famous book, which you may not have read, which chiefly proves biologically, that by the year 3000 everybody will be born female. Liebele meine Schwesterli, no Jean Harlow, but the zippiest madcap I've known, the most fun to be with. I hired her to edit the Italian edition of *Perspectives (Prospetti)* and we circumcopulated Magna Graecia several times. I was keen to heirate her, but she could love only old men, because of their wisdom. Her first love was Silone, old enough to be her grampa; her husband was Giuseppe Antonio Borgese, who looked like an ancient elephant; next came Corrado Tumiatti, editor of the most intellectual magazine in Florence; and now she commutes around the world with a Maltese nonagenarian, president of the ocean institute, but she runs it. She is the one who taught her dog to type. Adriano Olivetti had a special typewriter built for him with big keys he could hit with his nose. He could type "Mi chiama Arli" and "aril ha fame" and various other bits of higher knowledge. She also had a chimpanzee but all he wanted to do was play with himself. She was the first girl to drive from Rome to New Delhi on a motorbike. She wanted me to accompany her but I didn't think I could take the heat. I don't think there is any point in my trying to do a segment of *Byways* on Schwesterli . . . nobody would believe it . . . she calls me Brooderli because I brood.

BORGESE, ELISABETH

At the Goethe Festival in Aspen the little daughters of
Elisabeth Borgese caused much discomfort to the scholars by
crawling under the doors of the stalls in the men's room of the
Hotel Jerome and locking them from the inside, and these
maidens also sprayed water from a hose on Doctor Schweitzer,
who smiled on them with his Christian agape, and your friend
Spender, who said they should be caned, and we told him he
was the one who knew how to do it, but he wouldn't and the
terror continued . . .

BOWLES, PAUL

Here is the documentation on the libelous lies of the hashish-eating scum-bag. . . .

There was never any question of a suit. The dogs'-behind-licker deserved chastisement for his behavior toward me, who had made him ex nihilo with my extraordinary promotion of *Sheltering Sky* through 7 printings, a script which was refused by every big publisher, including "Joke-book" Cerf. . . what was I about to say? . . . oh yes, the vomit-drinker behaved in Dishonorable and Contemptible fashion but he did nothing that was technically illegal.

The amount cited is ridiculous. 20 times such a figure would be nearer correct. Longfang will certainly have Price Waterhouse search my old checks. The obliquious snot-sniffer deserves my wrath, but I won't stoop to his level. The truth is he has had a miserable life of his own making. But when my auto-bug-offery appears it will reproduce in facsimile Tenn's letter affirming that dribble-pisser has the most minute membrun non-virile he has ever seen.

Over in India, where you ought to be, too. The letter explaining the missing of the boat never arrived, I can tell you. I managed to get my return passage put off until April 25th, so I had the time to come. The Cape is a wonderful spot to work and bathe. Not much else, of course, as it is unfrequented and the village consists of fishermen's huts and three or four shops and a very large Hindu temple with bathing ghats, all directly on the sea. The sun is vicious, and I got dreadfully burned by it. With such a strong, cool wind one doesn't realize how strong it is itself, and of course the latitude is such that the damned orb is directly overhead in the middle of the day. That is my news. That and the fact that I finally visited Madura temple, which was worth the god-awful trip I had to make to get there. Also that Laughlin cabled he was suing me. He is in Switzerland skiing. Suing my agent, to

be exact. I have written him various times saying that I don't understand why. Either one has done something illegal or not. I imagine I shall hear soon from the agent, saying to worry or not to worry. Yes, Touche said you had fallen in love . . . . .

. . . . .

than one minute ahead. I'm trying to write a book, and finding it a bore. Perhaps it's the heat. I'd rather do anything than try to think of those damned characters, who are automatically boring because I'm writing about them. Probably, too, they're boring people anyway, or I shouldn't be writing about them. I really have no interest in writing books if all one can get out of one which has been on the best-seller lists as long as *Sky* has, is $337.50. I thought I could make two or three thousand dollars, but it just isn't so. There's absolutely no money in it. Fortunately I'm not starving, as I brought some

FROM THE THREEPENNY REVIEW WINTER 1993

Paul Bowles   The Sheltering Sky

BOOKISHNESS

Before I got to Choate with Fitts, my reading was mostly in the Bible. My grandfather gave us passages to memorize and if we got them right we would get a shiny new dime. I think that I enjoyed the standard boy books, *Robinson Crusoe*, and that sort of thing. I still have some of them here upstairs if you want to look at them. Most of them were illustrated very colorfully by a fellow named Wyeth. When I was about 12, I started writing little blank verse plays for my cousins whom I coerced into putting into production in one of the relative's houses. My parents had a "decorative" library of standard authors. That means that there were glass cases in the big living room in Pittsburgh which served instead of wallpaper. The only person who looked at them was the parlor maid who dusted them. Yes, I've always been bookish.

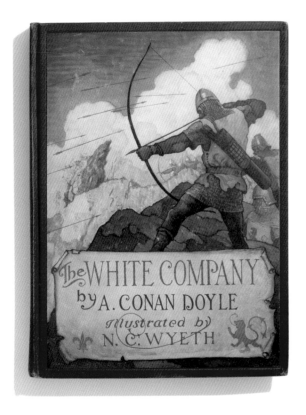

BROWN UNIVERSITY

J is still working hard correcting the last batch of papers
from his course, concentrating on each one as though he was
about to send it to the printer. I particularly liked his comment
to one lazy girl who didn't proofread her paper. "Would
you wear a spotted dress to a party?"

ANN LAUGHLIN
TO JACK AND
SOPHIE HAWKES

My students range from tops to, well, what do you think of this little miss, who ended her paper: "We cannot say that Pound's 'Mauberley' is a work of art because he writes about so many people in Greece and Rome who nobody knows anything about any more. Pound could not have written this poem without Froula's guide."

The course is going okay, except none of the girls will talk.
Lorrie says they are in "awe" of me. I'm going to have office
hours to get some awe out of them. (But will leave
the door open.)

BURKE

Do you know Kenneth Burke? We went out there to interview
him for the WCW dokuku. 88 and all bent over but what an
ouragon of passion for ideas and language. He's lived on the
same farm in New Jersey for over 60 years. His daughters made
him put in plumbing but he still uses the old privy in summer.
Pages from learned journals for bumwad. And I have
shat / where that great mind sat.

BUNTING

We were just over in England for two weeks and got some very fine stuff for the Pound documentary. One of the most interesting interviews was with Bunting, for which we had to go all the way up to Newcastle. He is really a fascinating man. He told me a lot of things that I never heard before, if he was not making them up. For example, he said that Ezra had told him that "Mauberley" was a hoax, the idea inspired by some kind of hoax which Samuel Butler pulled, but I haven't gotten to the bottom of that. I wonder which Butler book it would be. Bunting was also interesting on the subject of Whitman, claiming that he had an enormous influence on some of Ezra's metric and rhythms. Previously, I had always thought that Ezra dismissed Whitman with the little poem we both know, but perhaps Bunting is right. This bears looking into.

The reason that I never published Bunting, whose work I greatly admire, was that he thought I was a capitalist viper and would not send me anything or let me reprint. Actually, I found him absolutely delightful the day that we interviewed him for the film at Hexham. He'd talked a blue streak of funny anecdotes until the bottle of good scotch ran out, and then he lowered his head onto his chest and went sound asleep.

BREADKNIVES

I propose to do a poem on "The bread knife which cuts thru 8 loaves at once" but it will take a lot of thought.

BIG SPRINGS

I told you about "glup" didn't I? When I was about ten, my brother and Jack Heinz, both older, were chums. They liked to build dams on our "farm" Big Springs in the mountains near Rolling Rock. (It was called Big Springs because a powerful spring gushes out of the mountains, making pools and trout streams.) Jack said we must have a company to do this. And he formed, with documents, "Hans, Gluppel & Glup." He was Hans, and Hugh was Gluppel, and I was little Glup. Hans and Gluppel had all the best fun, finding stones and putting them together. All Glup was allowed to do was to fetch glup, pieces of sod which made Glup's hands bloody, wresting them from the meadow, and toting them to his masters. "More glup, Glup," they would cry, "Get a move on, we need more glup."

80 Eighth Avenue   New York 10011   AL5-0230

Date:

Subject:

Big Springs
—

Hans Gluppel + Glup.
Old stage in
Spring House. Skinning clean
Papa casting for cigarettes
Theatra
Lloyd – Drunk but not
          Drunkard
             Tenseldom
the cornnuts
   haying
The raft + Daddy Bill
The pools + The nellows.
Th h emselves. Stonewalls.
Jackie's fallen down
             place
   The barn
   Sugaring Syrup.

It is a risk to be my friend. I operate on the principle that if someone does me a kindness that entitles me to ask immediately for another favor. That's not as immoral as it sounds – if you're a Buddhist. When I was working as a cultural boy scout for the Ford Foundation in Burma I learned a great, basic principle. If I'm a Buddhist and I ask you for a favor I'm conferring merit on you by allowing you to do a good deed. If you collect enough good deeds that will shorten the time it takes you to become a Bodhisattva. But it still may take a while to reach that grade; Buddhist time is gradual. It goes by kalpas. How long is a kalpa? My golfing pal U Khin Zaw, the head of Burmese Radio, explained it thus: every year a bird flies up to the top of Kanchenjunga and brushes his wing against a rock; when the mountain is worn away that is a kalpa.

I learned about merit collecting the hard way. My best friend in Rangoon was the painter U San Win. He had a smile like the Buddha himself. We used to sit meditating on his porch drinking Mandalay beer. The Foundation had given me a budget to encourage the painters so I bought one of his paintings. San Win decided that I was worthy of more merit and allowed me to give him my beautiful gold cufflinks. He was a dear man and I'm still feeling very meritorious.

The struggle for enlightenment is a dynamic process.

BURMA

WATER FESTIVAL

So we have had to endure Water Festival here, and endure is indeed the proper word. It goes on for five days and is a most disgusting spectacle of mass rowdyism. All work stops and everybody in town goes cruising all day around the streets in jeeps and trucks dowsing each other with water from squirt guns, buckets and fire hoses. They put barricades in the streets to stop the cars and if you don't open the windows to let them dowse you they break them open with rocks or sticks. The amazing thing is that grown up men go in for it just as enthusiastically as the kids. Two of my businessmen friends here, one the owner of the best newspaper and another the big coffee merchant, had hired trucks to go around in and seemed quite amazed when I declined their invitations to spend the day with them getting soaked. The extent of my voluntary cooperation in this mass release of repressions was to lunch at Professor Myo Min's and let his children give me a going over. But this was rather fun as it was done in a nice spirit. The wetting was followed by the traditional Thingyam lunch of scented rice, rotten fish soup, decayed prawn sauce, and a nasty dessert of fruit jello swimming in coconut milk. I'm afraid I just never will get to like Burmese food. It isn't as hot as Indian food, but it smells much horrider. My formula, when I have to eat it, is to gulp it down with large quantities of Mandalay beer.

CORSO, GREGORY

GJO—a rather drunken but good humored call from Corso in Colorado. He asked me if I would leave him my teeth in my will so he could have a good mouth. What he seems really to want is to take out a poem and put in another in the next printing of his book. He also objects to one line on the back ad. I asked him to write it to you. He said we could charge his royalties for the changes.

CULTURAL WASTELAND: U.S.A.

Remember the writing that Belshazzar saw on the wall
MENE MENE TEKEL UPHARSIN

THAT CUBAN

That Cuban is odd.
He put the heat
up to 90, and when
he ate he dunked
his BLT in the soup.

CANDLEWOOD, WILLIAM

He used to write rejection letters to authors. He was also the whipping boy. If something fouled up at New Directions it was always blamed on Candlewood. The apology letters said he would be fired immediately.

FICTITIOUS CHARACTER NAMED FOR CANDLEWOOD LAKE, CT.

CHILDREN

We have two chipmunks in a box. They do smell mightily, but are instructive for youth, tho I fear youth is not always kind to them. I fear A. Schweitzer wd not approve. But my good mother says little folk must have pets. And besides they hopped of their own will into the garbage barrel. Life is full of choices, and it is hard to choose the right thing, for oftimes what first appears right, is not ultimately so.

COCTEAU

I wish that nice Marse Jean Cocteau were still around. He took me to lunch at the Grand Véfours in the Palais-Royal and explained clearly all about flying saucers. He understood mechanical things. He would advise me. He was amiable.

CLINTON

My library is now complete. I have been given the Treasure of Treasures. The other day UPS delivered a box from the Maison Blanche. It contained a magnificently produced picture book, about 10 x 20", entitled *Clinton: Portrait of a Victory.* The inscription reads: "For Jim / with my heartfelt thanks / Bill." All the photos were taken during the campaign by the head photographer of *Time,* who was apparently allowed to follow him around everywhere, almost into bed with Hilary. There is one sweet picture where she is on the sofa (the upstairs parlor) cuddling his tired head in her lap, comforting him after a hard day. There is a good one too where he is holing a chip shot on the golf course. Many of these pictures are good as photos, Kunstfotos.

I had sent him a modest contribution because I liked his smile and his oratory. I thought to myself: here is a president who is not a slimy politician like George. He loves the downtrodden peepul and he will find ways to improve their lot. He won't start a war, like George. Poor Smiley, he has had a lot of bad breaks, and made a lot of goofs, or his staff has made them for him. Those miserable senators—Dole is the worst—are creaming him and making him look foolish. He loves the sound of his manly voice talking, and often he talks before he has thought. The press enjoys making sport of him. Many of his staff—kids from the campaign—are inexperienced in the tricks of the "Beltway." I've not given up hope. Virtue will triumph in the end . . .

Intolerable gossip. I heard two ladies from out of town discussing our leaders, that Hilary is a dyke and Smiley is having an affair with Barbra Streisand. O tempora! Obviously embittered Republicans.

CARSON, ANNE

*When I first read the "God poems" in the magazine, I had a kind
of pleasant and electric shock thinking that you were the
poet I had been waiting for for some years.*

She is a Volcanist; she paints volcanoes that look like the sundaes we used to get at the drugstore counters exploding with chocolate sauce. I shouldn't be irreverent. She's obviously someone to be reckoned with.

She's taken leave of the mundane world in her work and it's more than delightful. It's slightly frightening. One asks oneself have I lost the lid off my head?

*Dear G, I'm sad and despondent. See her letter, Anne Carson
is flirting with some lady at Knopf for the next book. I thought
I had disposed of Knopf. Before I did her book I asked if her
contract with Knopf gave them an option / She said no. Then
I had Peggy (please check) put in an option for us. Does this
carry any weight? I don't want to fuss with AC. You've met her,
how serious do you think she is about this move? What's up? I
see that I offered her $2500. Is it likely that Knopf would top that
for poetry? Do you know this Amy Scheibe well enough to ask?
I'm innocent of such procedures. I don't want to hassle with her.
Drop the book rather than that. I'd rather have a friend than a
discontented poet. Should you pick up on the negotiations?
I want to be lighthearted with her. Tell her that I'll be 82 in Oct,
that she is the star of ND, and I'd like to have another amble in
that paradise garden. From the day I read her God poems
in the APR I knew she was our star. Sorry to dump this on you,*

Thanks, J

CÉLINE

The terrifying French novelist, Louis Ferdinand Céline—an enormously powerful and slashing, satiric, misanthropic writer. But what power of the imagination! We did three books of his. He was overpowering.

My friendship with Céline was curious. He was a fascist and an anti-Semite. He wrote some hideous anti-Semitic books. I didn't buy any of that, but I was fascinated by the power of his writing. He had to flee from France, because of his connection with the Vichy French, and he was living in Denmark. His wife was a ballet dancer, but she couldn't get any proper ballet shoes in Denmark. So Céline would write to me about every two or three months, asking me please to go to Capezio's and get some more size six and airmail them over for his beloved. That was how I first got in contact with him directly. I had made the arrangement for doing his greatest books, *Journey to the End of Night* and *Death on the Installment Plan*, through his publisher. But I did meet him later. He was allowed to return to France, and was exonerated of his supposed crimes. Yet he lived in terror, because his French publisher had been assassinated as a collaborator on the street in Paris. Céline was then living near the Renault plant outside of Paris. I went to see him there. It was a little villa with high barbed wire all around it. There were two very fierce dogs on guard. Céline and his wife were friendly, but he wouldn't talk about himself, though I had asked him to recall his days working in a factory in the United States.

JOURNEY TO

THE END OF

THE NIGHT

CÉLINE

lustig + quigley

CARRUTH, HAYDEN

The way Hayden got to know me so well is this. I first met him when I stopped by the Chicago office of *Poetry*, which he was editing. We hit it off. When he left *Poetry* I brought him to the Ford Foundation Intercultural Publications office to help me edit *Perspectives*. But he developed a strange condition. If there were more than four people in the office he would begin to shake. Twice he fainted in the subway. His family enrolled him in the Bloomingdale cracker-factory in White Plains. He was there about a year. When he got out I invited him up here to Norfolk and put him in a cottage on the place. Half the time he wrote (he published a book called *The Norfolk Poems*), half the time he worked on ND stuff, reading scripts, writing blurbs, etc. One great job he did was organization of the files. All the ND letters from the earliest years were just piled up in cartons. Reading all those letters I suggested he make some notes toward a history of ND. He put his reading into an 86-page account, which he never finished because Eros called.

One summer Ann's sister Helen and 7 children were residing in the big house, my Aunt having gone to Heaven, or, as she put it, "on to greater understanding." To look after the children Helen had imported an English-speaking au pair from East Germany. The minute Hayden saw her his romantic heart fibrillated. He took her riding in his battered autocar, recited his poetry, and hurled the bardic gaze into her entranced orbs. They were engaged in a fortnight. I don't think Hayden sedulated her. He was always a very upright person. Besides he was then timid with girls because he had gone through a traumatic experience.

A certain well-known blonde and comely poet (she is still extant and fairly famous so I won't name her) kept him locked in a room of The White Hart Inn in Salisbury, and, a veritable Messalina, she had her way with him again and again. For lack of food, though she did bring up a few sandwiches, and mounting terror, the sensitive young man passed out.

The Salisbury Volunteer Firemen had to revive him with oxygen. I told the lady poet she had better leave Connecticut quick; we don't go for her type.

So Rosemarie and Hayden were married by the local JP (himself a literary man who wrote essays for the *Atlantic*). They went up to Vermont where they found an ancient farmhouse which I helped them acquire.

Dear Hayden,

Can it be that I've never answered your August letter? Time rushes along, toward Death (there's a cheerful note!) and I don't seem to get much done. Who wrote Oblomov? *I seem to sleep a lot, except at night when, like Delmore, I get insomnia.*

Jas,

I don't know who this three-piece editorial type is that you've installed in the "white cottage," I don't even know where or what the white cottage is (since I presume it isn't the one I was living in thirty-odd years ago), but truly, whoever he is, he is NOT the person to show Byways *to. Very few people are. What you are doing has never been done before; Wordsworth, Wally Stevens, and Derrick Walcutt do not, rpt. do not, give the Literati the clue they need to perceive and appreciate what you are up to. So do not be discouraged by anything coming from those quarters.* **Das ist verboten.**

CHILDHOOD

How did you know that I tore the hands off grandfather's clock? William Buffalo, the #2 chauffeur, glued them back on. There were no child psychiatrists in 1920. My Mother took it to the Lord in prayer. I was whupped of course.

Another early memory of Pittsburgh that will never leave me was my terror of kidnappers. Several children of rich families were kidnapped. Two were gotten back with ransoms but one was murdered; the body was found in the woods of Frick Park. We heard about these horrors from the Irish maids. One of the health fads of those days was sleeping porches. It was thought that colds and tuberculosis could be avoided if one breathed fresh air while sleeping. Of course the air of Pittsburgh was filthy then with the smoke from the steel mills. If it snowed in the night the snow would be dark gray by noon. Air conditioning was unknown. If windows had to be opened in summer the maids fitted wooden frames with cheesecloth on them into the windows. These would be gray by evening. The cheesecloth was changed and washed by Minnie the laundress down in her laundry in the basement. (The basement had its own life. There were two enormous furnaces with huge boilers, two in case one went on the blink. There was a wine-cellar room which was kept locked so we children couldn't get into it. There was a room full of split pinewood sent up from Sydonie for the fireplaces. Mother had a bulb room where she raised narcissus and hyacinths in wet pebbles; she started them at different times so there were blooms for the rooms upstairs in sequence. Father had his game room where ducks, wild turkeys and sometimes a deer hung from hooks in the ceiling until they were "ripe" to eat. Most curious was the egg room where eggs were stored in water to keep them fresh. Better than the icebox.)

CHILDHOOD

ALL OF A SUDDEN PEGGY

. . . I went to Arnold, not Shady Side, and there was a play called "All of a Sudden Peggy," in which I was the female lead. It was presented in an auditorium at Tech, which had a Theater department run by a very elegant Englishman. He got angry with me because there was food in one scene—creamed chicken—which I gobbled hungrily, forgetting that I had lines to say . . .

People always warn that I'll trip over my untied shoelaces and have a bad fall. That only happened once. We were in New York visiting various relatives. I tripped and fell right in front of the Vanderbilt Hotel. It was a bad one. I was cut so deep I had to be taken to the hospital emergency room and have stitches. This made us late getting to Aunt Patty's lunch party at the Vanderbilt which put her in a pet. What I did in the hotel dining room made her furious. It was the first time I had ever had an oyster. It tasted horrible and I spat it out right on the floor. Mother took me up to Aunt Patty's bedroom and gave me the hairbrush. And that was the end of the ten dollar goldpieces that used to come from Aunt Patty every Christmas.

I won't bore you with any more shoelace stories, except for one. We were in London on one of our summer trips "to acquire cultivation" as they called it. Mother was off in the country visiting a school friend, so my brother and I were alone with father. He said he was tired of the Burlington Hotel dining room, he would take us to his club. That's what he called it, "his club." It was a house in Bulstrode Street, nothing that would tell you from the outside it was anything but some family's

house. A butler let us in and took
us to the second floor in a small
elevator. We were greeted in the
sitting room by a handsome lady
who looked somewhat like the Queen.
All dressed up. She and father
seemed to be friends. They kissed.
We didn't sit down but the queen
lady went out and came back with
the most beautiful girl I had
ever seen. "This is Winifred," the
Queen said, she'll entertain you
young men for half an hour. Then
she and father went off somewhere.
Winifred was a princess for sure,
she was wearing a rather scanty
dress but it was made of gold.
This was many years ago but
I can still see how lovely she was.

And she was nice. "What will it be, gentlemen," she asked, "chess or checkers?" Neither of us had ever heard of chess, so we said checkers. As she was going to get the checkers set she noticed my untied shoelace. "Dear me," she said, "your man doesn't take very good care of you, does he?" And if you'll believe it (I still can't) this gorgeous princess knelt right down on the floor beside me and did up not one, but redid both of my laces. Then we played checkers and the butler brought us ginger and bitters, as he called it. I suppose I should have been embarrassed, but I wasn't. I'll never forget her or our visit to the house in Bulstrode Street.

Luminous Detail:
outside the arena gladiators wear tailored
silk purple sweatsuits with "game cocks"
embroidered in gold.

CUMMINGS, E.E.

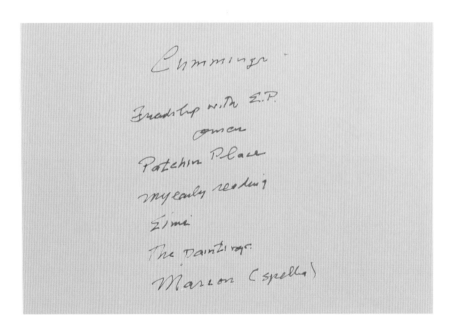

And there is Cummings's nice
"may I feel said he / I'll squeal said she."

For me, Cummings is the heir in our time of the Elegiac Poets, crossed with Martial, and of Herrick and Rochester. Like Dylan Thomas, he was the master of the great first line. Pound urged everyone to read *Eimi*, the prose book about Russia. I found it tedious and much prefer *The Enormous Room*. Pound probably liked *Eimi* because it is anti-Communist. Strange that he should have approved of word-play prose when he so hated *Finnegans Wake*.

It was a fine reward for a day's work at the office, which was then in the old triangular building at the corner of Sixth Avenue and 4th Street, when the Cummingses would ask me to drop by for tea in Patchin Place. They were in Number 4 on the ground floor, with Djuna Barnes, whom they mothered with chicken broth when she was poorly, upstairs. The Cummingses lived a rather self-contained life. I seldom saw them around the Village. Marion, who was a fine photographer, was tall and very beautiful. She had once been a fashion model. She was serene but with her special sparkle. Estlin was on the small side, wirey, but even though he seldom left his armchair I felt the energy coming out of him. He talked with a Yankee twang; his eyes seemed to talk as well as his mouth. He wasn't a raconteur, but what he said was always pithy and witty. His laugh had a little cackle in it, not unlike Bill Williams's Jersey cackle. They had been friends for years.

Cummings's relaxation was painting. There were always a number of oils in the apartment, often changing. I was never greatly taken with his work, but it meant ever so much to him. And I don't forget that when Pound was brought to Washington from Italy for trial Cummings sent the thousand dollars for which he had sold a painting to the defense fund. (Hemingway did the same.)

PRIZE-WINNING ESSAYS

1931 1932

Atlantic Essay Contest for High School Students

● ● ●

FIRST PRIZE
$50

Salle D'Étude
By
James Laughlin

The Choate School,
Wallingford, Connecticut
Dudley Fitts, *Teacher*

SECOND PRIZE
$25

Storm Wings
By
Lindsay A. Fowler

The Choate School,
Wallingford, Connecticut
Dudley Fitts, *Teacher*

THIRD PRIZE
$10

Alleys
By
Annette MacDonald

The Lewis and Clark
High School,
Spokane, Washington
Marian Pettis, *Teacher*

●

HONORABLE MENTION

Nocturne

By
Charles Homer Newton

The Choate School,
Wallingford, Connecticut
Dudley Fitts, *Teacher*

Time Tables

By
Annette MacDonald

The Lewis and Clark
High School,
Spokane, Washington
Marian Pettis, *Teacher*

**Youth Looks at
Religion**

By
Beverly Lyon

Lowell High School,
San Francisco, California
William J. Gannon, *Teacher*

The method of entering essays in the contest becomes of particular interest when one school wins three prizes and one student is awarded Third Prize and Honorable Mention. On receipt of the essays the instructor's endorsement and the names of the student and school are removed and the essays assigned numbers. The judges of the contest are therefore entirely unaware of the identity of the writers or their schools until after the prize-winning essays have been chosen.

THE ATLANTIC MONTHLY

ington Street   Boston, Massachus

May 18

Received word of winning Atlantic
monthly Essay contest with *Seldes*
D Steele and received as well
check for $50. Spent as follow:

				50.00
1.	Dettes, Joseph: Don Juan	.65	49.28	
2.	Lawrence: St Mawr American			
	First edition	$2.00	47.20	
3.	additional on above	14¢	47.06	
3.	Duff. Chas: "James Joyce and			
	The Plain Reader.	80¢	46.26	
4.	Mencken: Style and Form in			
	American Prose	81¢	45.45	
5.	D H Lawrence: Touch and Go	1.80	1.80	
	First Eng Edition		43.65	
6.	Kay Boyle: Year Before Last	2.50	2.50	
	First Am Edition		41.15	
7.	Gilbert: Joyce's "Ulysses"	3.50	3.50	
	Slightly defaced		37.65	
8.	Little Review Feb 1918 Ezra		.80	
	Pound: French Poets		36.85	
9.	Fitts: Two Poems (signed)		.60	
	Pamphlet of Modern Edit, no limit		36 - 25	
10.	museum of modern arts		1.55	
	Catalogue of murals.		35.10	

UPON WINNING
THE FIFTY DOLLAR
FIRST PRIZE IN
THE ATLANTIC
ESSAY CONTEST
FOR HIGH SCHOOL
STUDENTS, JL
NOTED HOW HE
SPENT THE MONEY
ON BOOKS

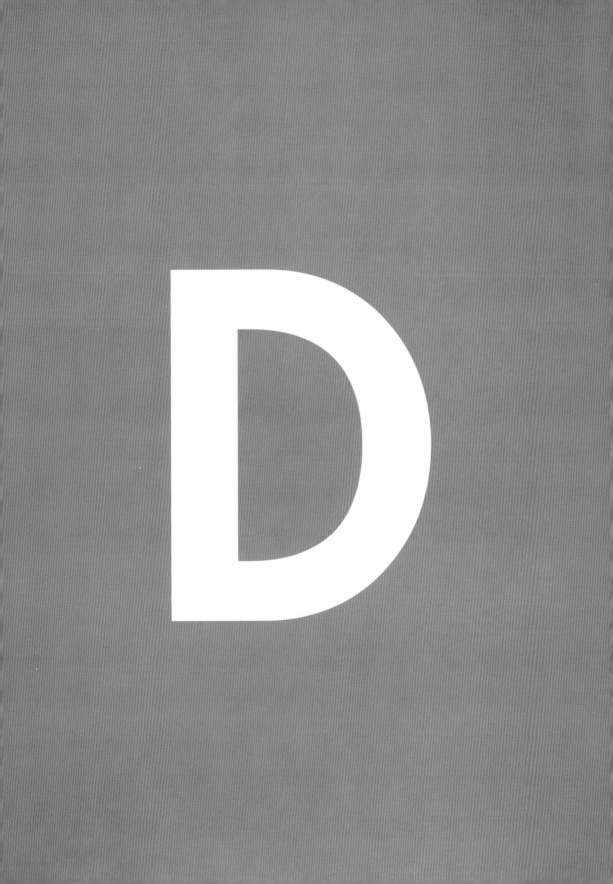

DAHLBERG

DREADFUL EDWARD

I should have spotted from something he said when I first took him out to lunch that Edward Dahlberg was going to be a problem. Over a BLT on 4th Street (no New Directions author has ever been lunched at the Four Seasons) Edward told me, quite seriously, that Edmund Wilson was "a very ignorant man."

DAVENPORT, GUY

PARIS REVIEW INTERVIEW

When *Tatlin!* was accepted for publication, I remember being anxious and frightened, truly frightened, that reviewers would say, "This is pretentious." What they said is, "This is obscene." I've gotten over that. I did feel ashamed that people would write some of the reviews I'd seen. I was explaining this to Laughlin once in a letter and he replied with an absolutely lovely sentence. The sentence is: "Never, read reviews." I think the comma may have been a mistake. Laughlin never mastered the typewriter at all. But somehow it's the most eloquent comma I have ever run across. Anyway, most reviews are useless.

DURRANCE, DICK

"I didn't know who Laughlin was or anything about him.
Skiing in New Zealand and Australia was not exactly the kind
of thing that everybody did in 1937. But the idea was so exciting
that I didn't hesitate very long. In fact what I said was yeah
yeah yeah." They were an unlikely Mutt-and-Jeff pair—J
was six-foot five, Durrance five-foot seven. (Or as Dave Bradley
described them, Brobdingnagian Laughlin, Lilliputian Durrance.)
J's father was well off; Dick was slinging hash in the mess
hall for his meals. But both were young and strong and had
great appetites for adventure, and both had developed a deep
love of big-mountain European skiing.

DICK
DURRANCE:
THE LIFE
AND TIMES OF
AMERICA'S
FIRST GREAT
SKI RACER

DENTISTS

I feel a slight burning sensation in a rear molar. I believe this is called empathy. It's a feeling I can easily adduce because I've had such a peculiar history with one of my upper fronts. A few years ago it started to fall out. Cause unknown. My dentist, who has built a new garage with the fees levied on my bridge, kept popping it back in with various supposedly sustaining gidgets. But it kept popping out. Most remarkable was an event long to be remembered in London literary circles when it popped out as I was at the height of my eloquence at a reading with Gavin Ewart and Peter Porter at a club devoted to the work of lady lesbian sculptresses. The tooth flew at least 20 feet in the air. There was astonishment and virginal applause. Soon little scurries were down on their knees hunting for it under the chairs. It was from this triumph that I met the young lady poet from Islington who asked me to agree that poems must be true to be beautiful.

DUNCAN, ROBERT

That great bard R. Duncan was here for the weekend and talked for 8 hours straight. His new poems are so beautiful. Nobody since EzPo can make like he can make with the words. And the music of ideas.

R. Duncan reported this nice Ez story. My name came up at St Liz and Ez declared: "Jaz has a very long spine and he is always breaking it skiing. So when I kick his butt about what he should publish, the message does not ascend to his brain."

DANIELOU, ALAIN

We both wanted to study to study the incredible spectacle of
ten thousand Hindus bathing in the filthy water of the Ganges
and drinking all of it they could swallow; the sight of the dead
bodies being burned on sandalwood pyres on the ghats along
the riverbank. And we had a date to call on Alain Danielou, the
Frenchman who had become a Hindu (although his brother
S.J. became a Roman cardinal), the great scholar of Sanskrit literature and Vedic music, the author of the Bollingen book on
the Hindu theogony; we visited him in his miniature Mughal
palace. There he was in his dhoti, sitting on a pile of silken
cushions, plucking out ragas on his sitar, a font of wisdom
about everything Indian.

DIVORCE

I have not meant to be this long in replying to your very moving letter of 1/31. Having been through that mill myself, my sympathy for all involved is very real and deep. I kept thinking I would get out my Pleiade Racine and therein find some couplet which eloquently tells of the tyranny of the human heart, or how futile it is to struggle against destinies we cannot comprehend. But will instead quote the wise words of Abe Yokum, boatman on the Snake River, Wyoming: "If you capsize, don't fight the current. Pull up your knees to your stomach. Keep your nose above water and wait till the current washes you ashore." I guess that's about the sum of my wisdom. But far greater is my sense of how rough it must be for you . . .

```
                                                          In youth
I was sullen & taciturn; in old age I'm mellow but babbling. My shrink
says I'm trying to put off death by blowing wind. Timor mortis conturbat
me. Bill kept telling me that when we were dead we were dead. I fear he
was right.
```

DEATH

This is a stupid letter. Most days the clocks have stopped and I breathe through the omphalos. Can you picture that? I'm a case of which the local medical men have washed their hands clean. Nobody knows why I go on ticking.

ECONOMICS

That dear little Mr. Perot never read Pound's *ABC of Economics*. He doesn't understand that the bankers and their sick friends would never let the national debt be retired. They would lose all that juicy interest.

EGYPT

Lambrose K. Lambrose, the mystery financier of Norfolk, says that a Nubian slave invented the gas engine and the pharaohs had a little cart. Should I believe him? I didn't see this cart depicted on the wall of the tomb in the Valley of the Kings.

EISENHOWER

AS YOU KNOW PRES EISENHOWER SUFFERED CRUELLY FROM DIVERTICULITIS, THOUGH WITH HIM I THINK IT WAS GRAPE SEEDS. I'VE ALWAYS LIKED IKE FOR THESE REASONS:

1. He did not cheat at golf the way George does.

2. He initialed the chit that the aide who was fired for accepting a vicuna coat took over, the chit that is, to Justice, suggesting that 12 years in St Liz was enough. Actually, the prime mover was Ann's brother-in-law, Gabe Hauge, Ike's speech-writer. One morning at breakfast I told him Ez's sad story, of which he had never heard. "That poor man, that's awful," he said, "maybe we can do something about that." And he did. But the bloody academics won't believe me because, I suppose, I don't have a PhD. They insist it was Archie, or Frost or Hem. And that fellow who was Sec of State did report that we were getting a bad rep in Yurrup, Christian Somebody.

3. When Ike was president of Columbia a delegation of profs waited upon him to tell him that a professor of Philosophy was needed. Ike just said: "Procure one!"

4. And in London (that beautiful chauffeur) he deduced that a game of bridge was just as good as fornication.

THE STAFF FOR MY
AMBLYOPIA
EYE OPERATION
BY DR. CLAUDE
WORTH, THE KING'S
PHYSICIAN,
AT BULSTRODE ST.

JL:

Wodder, Wodder!

Sister Olive:

Do you mean wotah, dear?

In a 1946 letter to Pound WCW says that TS Eliot is "vaginal stoppage" and gleet.

There is no evidence that Eliot and Williams ever agreed about anything except in their affection for Pound. They were poles apart. The publication of the *Waste Land* and its instant success was a kick in the stomach for Williams, who was beginning to formulate his theories of strictly American poetry, an "American idiom," of our language as she is spoke. Eliot, he felt, was a traitor to his American origin, contaminated by European traditions. In 1939 Williams wrote me: "I'm glad you like his verse; but I'm warning you, the only reason it doesn't smell is that it's synthetic. Maybe I'm wrong, but I distrust that bastard more than any writer I know in the world today. He can write, granted, but it's like walking into a church to me." Apparently, similar sentiments were reported to Russell Square; Faber & Faber did not publish Williams in England, and it took some fifteen years to find a publisher who would risk the ecclesiastical wrath.

Eliot's blurbs were superb. What most people don't know was how he spent days rewriting the texts of Ezra's prose books so that they made more sense. And let us not forget the time that Tennessee was in London and the parson wanted to meet him to talk about dramatic structure; he took us to the Garrick but what they talked about mostly was ballet dancers' calves. And the year he was teaching at Harvard and had a suite in Eliot House where he invited the students once a week. He put the plate of sandwiches on the floor in the middle of the room, the students being seated around the periphery, and they were all too shy to go for a sandwich, so they lasted the whole term. Sic loquitur sapiens. Did you know him? An absolutely decent and kind man. There was one problem in conversing with him. He spoke very slowly, even slower than R. Fitzgerald; there were long spaces between his phrases. I would think he had finished his sentences and burst in but he hadn't, there would be more to come. His goodness to me, the instruction he gave about publishing, can't be gauged. There are some thirty letters from him in the archive patiently encouraging and chiding. A great literary document has apparently been lost: Delmore's fabular account of the courtship of Vivienne in a punt on the Cam. Add that when the boy scholar published in the *New English Weekly* a proof that *The Family Reunion* was an allegory of Social Credit he sent me, in manu sue, a note that it was the "most interesting interpretation" he had seen. His dedication in a gift copy of his edition of *Huck Finn* reads: "T. S. Eliot of Missouri to Jas Laughlin of Idaho, 21/XI, 50." Surely this saintly man sits high up the line on the right hand.

FISHING

Too bad Daniel caught no fish. It's like that some days. They are there but not hungry—at least for what one offers. We have true socialism in USA. John Haverlich catches many more big ones—on worms—in the Blackberry, near the Texaco Station, put there by State of Conn, than the Hollenback Members catch—with their flies—theirs put in by the Club, trucked weekly from a hatchery in Rhode Island.

Some of my Trout Friends

describe actual fish situation

Remark Chic

FIRBANK

PRANCING NOVELIST

Firbank was a dandy affecting very elegant clothes;
he had dozens of shoes and waistcoats. To get variety he liked
to wear two dressing gowns at once.

He liked to laugh like a clock running down:
the most wicked laugh in London.

His favorite meal was chicken livers,
strawberries and champagne.

He was a heavy drinker but not a drunk.

He had what he called a "nervous apprehension
about life"; London or places where there were
many people quite paralysed him.

He loved solitude.

To one friend who wanted to talk about literature
he said "I *adore* italics, don't you, Don't you?"

He was handsome but had a strong profile which Osbert Sitwell
described as "waving in and out with the line of a seacoast."

He told Sigfried Sassoon, "I am Pavlova, chasing butterflies"
to which Sassoon replied, "You are Tolstoy digging for worms."

As a boy Firbank wandered alone in the fields.
It was his way of keeping his personality whole.

His characters are isolated in self-absorption.

He strove to work out a form by which he could
convey the inner reality of his characters. Died 1926.

FAMILY

Did I write you that your namesake had gotten hold of
a bucket of bright yellow paint somewhere and had decorated
the large hemlock in the middle of the driveway so that it looks
like a perpetual Christmas tree? His mother says that he is
just "expressing himself" and that this is a good thing. The only
trouble is that he is also beginning to teach his younger brother,
Henry, also to express himself. One of these days I think that
poppa is going to express himself with a hairbrush. I suppose
this is all routine to you and Sally, but in the long lapse since
Paul and Leila were that age I had forgotten just how it was.

My daughter can make cross eyes crosseder than a Kabuki actor.
She also has a neat, logical mind and will go far. In response to
the question on the form: "Why do you wish to go to boarding
school?" she responded firmly: "I wish to learn to board."
Did we ever understand life so well?

FUNERALS

I hope your illness is over. It's a shame you had to miss a really
great funeral. I favor abortion for all, but those Catholics sure
know how to do it right with their ritual. My only beef was
the mass in English. I solved that for myself by intoning the
"In paradisum te deducant angeli" under my breath.

FITTS, DUDLEY

Were it not for Dudley Fitts, my English master at Choate, I would never have become a scribbler, nor for that matter a publisher. For it was Fitts, in correspondence with Pound, who arranged for me to study at the "Ezuversity" in Rapallo. And Pound, descrying no talent for poetry, ordained that I become a publisher.

Fitts was a handsome but slightly odd-looking man. He couldn't see much without his horn-rimmed glasses, but that wasn't it. Finally, as I observed him in class, it came to me. His forehead. His brow was higher by three eighths of an inch than that of anyone else in the room. He was indeed a highbrow.

My first brief conversation with him is forever etched, as they say, on the plate of memory. As an underformer I had seen him around, but had never been assigned—we were rotated every two weeks—to his table in the dining hall. One day when I was rushing up the stairs from the mail room and he was coming down wearing the black Dracula cape which he affected, I bumped into him and knocked him half down. The irate gaze of Hermes was fixed upon me and he uttered: "You young puppies who haven't even read Thucydides!" And the God continued on his errand.

Jay will not, I think, write the American Ulysses. *He will not, so far as I am now able to judge, write anything but the world's rudest letters.*

FITTS TO
FITZGERALD
1934

It is a pleasure, Robert, to publish you, who do not squawk, yatter and produce shit hemorrhages on the office rug, and it will be a great glory after one is dead.

FITZGERALD, ROBERT

On the wall of my dressing room there is an enlarged photograph of two old geezers riding in a golfcart. The photographer has caught them in the middle of a conversation. What are they talking about? The fine golf shots and long putts they've made? No, they're talking about Homer. One of the golfers knows all there is to know about Homer; he is Robert Fitzgerald, the translator of the *Iliad* and the *Odyssey* (and also of Virgil's *Aeneid*). The other is one of his publishers who has been struggling for over fifty years trying to learn Greek but, having spread his life in six directions, has never managed to accomplish it.

FORD FOUNDATION

Bob Weil, the enlightened president of Macy's, who had Mortimer Adler, the University of Chicago philosopher, come to the store to lecture the younger executives on Aristotle so they would function more intelligently; Bob, who was one of my directors of Intercultural Publications which The Ford Foundation had set up in 1952 for me to do boy scout cultural work in various benighted countries such as India; Bob, a good egg who having heard that booze was forbidden in Bharat, had prepared for our trip by having Mark Cross, the purveyors of fancy luggage in New York, make up two large flat flasks that fitted into an elegant leather briefcase, which he told the customs man at the Delhi airport was not vodka but pure spring water needed for his diarrheic bowels, which the official believed and passed him through with a salute. And our next stop after we had checked in for a few days was the Foundation office, where I made smile contact with a beautiful little clerk named Rani, that's about all you can do with a good Brahman girl. The Foundation was mostly working to improve Indian agriculture. Doug Ensminger, the boss for the sub-continent, thought that Bob and I were pretty queer ducks, what the hell were we really up to, maybe we were spies from the administration to check up on his operation; but we had Rating-A credentials from the all-highest, Paul Hoffman, to investigate how the Commies circulated so many propaganda books in India; it didn't take us long to discover that they gave free bicycles to young men who had been through college but could find no jobs, then they gave them the books for free letting them keep most of the money. So Doug cleared us with Indian Intelligence and got us travel papers, but he thought it wise to give us a google-eyed ex-journalist named Kunhikrishnan, who turned out to be a very decent chap with a sense of humor about Indian customs, to help with our travel arrangements and, of course, to send in daily reports on what we were up to.

FAY, BERNARD

I would probably never have met Gertrude [Stein] if her best friend Bernard Fay had not found me appealing at the Schwimmban in Salzburg and had Gerturde invite me to Bilignin. A perfect gentleman, Monsieur Fay: several good dinners and invitations to his fashionable literary parties in the rue des Saints Peres, but never a problem. . . . The first real attempt on my person was made about 1941 in St. Louis where I was selling New Directions books to the stores.

When Bernard Fay came down for weekends from Paris there really was conversation. The two old friends knew each other so well they could play off each other's interests and eccentricities. It was a pleasure to hear the duet. Alice and I just listened. But an exchange I heard one night troubled me. They got on the subject of Hitler, speaking of him as a great man, one perhaps to be compared with Napoleon. How could this be? The Führer's persecution of the Jews was well publicized in France by that time. Miss Stein was a Jew and Fay had nearly gotten himself killed fighting the Boches. I couldn't forget that strange exchange. But later it came into sharper focus, at least in respect to Fay.

Apparently, as with some other intellectuals, he believed that the political chaos in France was destroying her culture. He opted for authoritarianism and after the collapse became a collaborator with Vichy. He was rewarded with the post of director of the Bibliothèque Nationale, later to be tried and sentenced to a long term in one of the island fortresses. Happily, for there was much to admire about him as a scholar and wit, he survived his imprisonment. And we doubtless owe the survival of Miss Stein and Alice during the war to Bernard Fay.

FICTION

My fiction tolerance stops with
The Good Soldier. Rexroth said,
"Jim, only children read novels."
And Griselda published Christine
Brooke-Rose's *Texterminations*
which I'll send. I think it's
about "the text doesn't know
what it's doing."

FROST, ROBERT

Robert
Frost +
Oscar
Williams.

FERLINGHETTI

Before I die I'd like to discover another rip-snorter—you know, like Ferlinghetti!

FATHER

Once in Boston—he kept an apartment in the Backbay for occasional visits all the years I was in Harvard—he put on his tuxedo one night and crashed a debutante party at the Hotel Somerset. I was mortified but the girls liked it, he was such a superb dancer and his manners so old-world. Another time, this in Miami, when we were in a nightspot with a very long bar lined with drinkers he took a running dive at one end slid on his stomach all the way to the other end knocking off all the drinks. Again, applause for the stunt; he ordered two rounds for all, he had such a way with him. Outrageous, and dipped in charm.

One of the passions of his later life was fishing. I say "later" because as long as James II was alive he put in time very regularly at Jones & Laughlin, first supervising the electrification at the new Aliquipa works down the Ohio (he had taken a degree in electrical engineering at Princeton) and then running the company coal mines up-river. But hardly was James II interred in Allegheny Cemetery but my father closed up his office at the company and embarked on a career of gentlemanly sport: Fishing (stream and deep sea), bird-shooting (there was special room in the basement at Woodland Road where the feathered bodies hung as they ripened), fast cars, yachting, golf (he played to a 6 handicap), and the pursuit on two continents of oiselettes, whom he always treated with liberality and kindness.

Papa beard Lincoln when manic

My father was an expert automobilist. Once in 1902 in a 5-mile race in Frick Park (Pittsburgh) (there were two men in each car, a driver and a mechanic), an important wire fractured from vibration and the vehicle came to a halt. My father seized the ends of the wire in each hand, allowing the current to pass through his body. The driver cranked up, leapt back to his seat, grasped the guide bar (this was before steering wheels), the engine sputtered, the car darted forward, and the race was won.

FATHER

I've left for the last an item of extravagance which affected me. One day when I was just past fourteen my father suggested that we go down to Florida. "What's the point," I asked, "when grandfather's place has been sold to the missionaries for a boarding school?" "Trust me," he said, "you'll be surprised." So we took the train and got off at Daytona, which has a very big beach where the sand is so hard that cars can race on it. Was he going to go in for racing? Not at all. We took a taxi to the marina, which is not on the ocean but on the inland waterway which runs down the whole eastern coast of Florida. We walked out on the pier and there amid the other boats that were tied up was a beautiful little cabin cruiser. My father walked up to it and told me to get aboard. "It's yours, Mate, and it's named Sarsho, which means fish in Seminole language." I burst out crying at such a gift. It turned out that the Sarsho had been designed by my father. He showed me his sketches, explaining various points. "But there's one thing you must promise me. This is light construction. You must never take it out into the ocean. Big waves might break it up." It wasn't a large boat, only about thirty feet from stem to stern, but it had everything just right to accommodate two people.

The Florida inland waterway isn't exactly beautiful. Mile after mile, the banks are thick mango swamp, except where there are scattered negro houses. But the bird life is wonderful, every kind of water bird you can think of. And the silence, pervasive silence. And the clouds drifting along overhead. We had enough canned food in the boat's frig till we came to the waterside town of Stuart. The mosquitoes were bad but we managed to sleep when we were anchored along the bank at night. In the noon heat we'd anchor to skinny-dip and then sunbathe on the forward deck. We'd heard tales of water moccasins but didn't see any. We spotted one alligator but he was asleep on a palm log and didn't budge. My father was patriotic: every morning he'd raise an American flag and a Princeton flag in the stern.

GREED

Camus, when I first wrote to him about doing his Caligula, said: "Je vois que vous n'êtes pas épicier." How wrong he was. I like to come out ahead, eventually. Which recalls the magnificent Dylan Thomas which Mardersteig did for me at the Officina Bodoni in Verona. It was a selection of his best poems to that date (1949). We sold out 140 copies at $100. Today the dealers are asking $3500 for it. If only I had tucked away a boxful in the attic.

GIRLS

As you point out, there is a dichotomy in the girl/woman department. I think I explained it to you once. In Latin, the word *puella*, which means girl, is very beautiful-sounding, while the word for woman, *mulier*, is to my ear very ugly. That's all there is to it. I'm an object of scorn from the feminists anyway, so it hardly matters.

GILL, BRENDAN

Now what are we going to do about Brendan? He's a schmeick-ler: His theme song is "I'm forever blowing bubbles." Instead of finishing his Great American Novel, *Ars Inc*, he flies about the country bloating the egos of his pals. There was a banquet in New York for Updike and Brendan had loaded the head table with his chums. He spent so much time blowing witty bubbles for them, there were only five minutes left for the honoree to make his pitch. Then next I found him at that great cultural center, Amarillo, Texas, where there was a testimonial dinner for T. Boone Pickens, the cowboy reincarnation of the old Wall St. speculator Gould. There was Brendan to congratulate all of us Gulf Oil stockholders whom Mr. Pickens had so enriched with his agile manipulations. And now this evening, more "pret-ty bubbles in the air" to comfort us old fogies of the Signet as we face oblivion in the computer age. What engine is driving our dear Brendan? And why does he have to be driven anyway? Doesn't Brendan have everything already? Isn't he the emi-nence grise of *The New Yorker*? Isn't Mayor Koch going to appoint him the next vicar of the St. Bartholomew's Church? Didn't he even have an afternoon date with Jackie Onassis? What more does he want? Why does he say nice things about me? He knows I won't say anything nice about him. I think I've guessed his secret. Brendan goes for universal love. He wants to outdo Dustin Hoffman as Willie Loman in the next production of "Death of a Salesman."

Dear Brendan,

I've had a full life and I'm ready to go. (Not as full a life as yours, I've never held hands with Jackie.) But there is an unfulfilled longing. I want to be published in your great magazine. I can't wait to see what nice (or bad) things beautiful big-eyed Cynthia says about me, but I want to be published as ME-ME-ME.

I know you are irresistible to all the ladies in your office. Could you take Alice out to lunch at the Algonquin and tell her this is a great poem? Get a receipt and I'll gladly remit. Or if she doesn't want to be seen with you in public, bring her a tall red rose (or a little yellow one, as you think best) for her desk. Tell her it comes from an ancient poet who is dying of psithurism (which gives him "a whispering sound as of wind among the leaves" — Webster) who wants to go down to Erebus famous, clutching a copy of the magazine.

Please point out to her that I know Mr. Newhouse is rather conventional, so let's not embarrass him, I have not employed my usual taciturn metric but have typed it out as free verse with capitals and punctuation. Do this, dear Brendan, as a parting kindness to your old chum. If I have a remission and can stagger again onto the links I'll drive three balls into the pond on Number 7 so that you can win. I know how much winning means to you.

If you can't make it with the poem try her next week with the prose. You could hint it's really a prose-poem sort of like Gaspard de la Nuit. If a subtitle is needed for those of your readers who did not have yours and my educational advantages it could be something like "Conrad's Marlowe Rides Again" in "Defense of a Slandered Fair One."

GINSBERG

When Ginsberg (always tolerant and kindhearted) wanted to help a starveling young poet he might close his letter by saying: take my letter to the Phoenix Bookshop in Cornelia Street, they may give you as much as $25 for it.

Olga asked Allen Ginsberg if he was also buying conference T-shirts for *his* grandchildren. She was most lovable throughout.

Dear Allen,

*I had gotten so used to seeing you around New York in the
dhoti you brought back from Benares where you earned your
food by stoking the fires of sandalwood which were burning the
bodies of devotees of Krishna and Vishnu on the ghats of the
Ganges, with your long unkempt hair of a sadhu begging his bowl
through the alleys of the ancient holy city . . . when unexpectedly
you sat down beside me at the YMHA at a tiresome poetry
reading (was it Charles Bernstein battering our ears with his
logodaedaly?) when you arrived freshly barbered in a pin-stripe
business suit so that I didn't recognize you till the rays of your
goodness emanated to me. . . . Can you forgive me, Allen, for
spreading the story at dinner parties (singing for my supper) of
your leaving your poems by the milk bottles on the back stoop
of Dr. Williams in Rutherford? I know it's not true, but it's so
true to your legend. I hope I've not too greatly offended. When
the last film flickers through my soon-dead head may I see and
hear you again playing your little harmonium and chanting
the songs of Blake in your raspy voice there on the fifth-floor
walk-up in the East Village where the stinking toilet was down
the hall near the stairhead.*

Great poet, good man, adept of happy-making laughter,

I salute you.

GAYS

I have never been able to understand their doing what they do.

In Greek poetry there are poems about an elderly gent holding hands with a beautiful youth while they examine the sunset and that's very sweet. But there are a lot of other poems which are so bad that the Loeb translators won't put them in English but put them in Latin.

Catullus' poems on these doings are most unattractive.

Gertrude Stein told Hemingway that what women do together is beautiful but that what men do is disgusting. Hem swallowed that till he came in unannounced one day and heard sounds from upstairs.

I do not consider the tumescent mentula an artistic object. But I have been told otherwise.

And you will run into a story by Tenn (I forget the title) where the enamoured swain gives himself an enema before going to meet his love.

The whole matter of what Auden called "copotomy & sodulation" baffles me. I guess I'm very square.

HORROR NOTE: And Tchelitchew, who was a great artist, used to ask the Poet Charles Henri Ford if he had swallowed every drop.

I am not now, have never been, and do not expect to become gay. I admire Guy Davenport's exquisite (and chaste) drawings of young men but my reaction to them is wholly aesthetic. It goes without saying that some of my literary friends are gay. But we don't discuss the subject. I deny that I ever have been paranoid about gays. Growing up on Woodland Road in Pittsburgh I never heard anything about them. In Shadyside Church Sunday School we were never assigned the Songs of Solomon, though we did hear about Solomon suggesting he would cut the baby in half. There were no sermons from the pulpit on Sodom and Gomorrah, though there were frightening descriptions of the Fires of Hell.

To get to Arnold School from Woodland Road (I would have been about eleven then) I boarded the school bus down on Shady Avenue. One of the faculty, Mr. Wilder, a rather stern little man, was on the bus to keep order. One morning a boy who hated me (it was said that his grandfather had been sent to the boobyhatch for shooting a famous architect, so naturally he was mean) started teasing that I was a "fairy." Mr. Wilder got angry. "I'll have none of that kind of talk on my bus." I asked Mr. Wilder what the boy meant. "It's another word for 'Christer,'" he said. That satisfied my curiosity. At Arnold I was not much liked. I was aloof because I was busy earning the gold medal with the head of Thomas Arnold, the great British schoolmaster, on it. I was never the kind of boy to whom other boys confided anything. I knew no jokes and heard no jokes.

I realize now that when I got to Eaglebrook dear old Mr. Gammons, who gave me special time in his own room (we read *The Rape of the Lock* by Pope) used to look at me very intensely. There was a rumor he had been fired from another school — for drinking. When I reached Choate there was a creepy boy who tried to touch my mentula in the shower. I told him I would break his face if he ever did that again. It was at Choate that I finally learned the facts. Every year the Headmaster, who should have been a Shakespearean actor, gave two famous sermons, which were eagerly awaited by the snickering student body. One was about self-abuse and how it might lead to the madhouse. The other, even better, was the "honest sailor" story. A sailor from the USS *Pensacola* then docked at the Brooklyn Navy Yard, called the "Head" because he felt it was his duty to tell him that Mr. R, a French master at Choate, had picked him up in a bar, tried to get him drunk and offered him money to perform a vile action. Mr. R left by the next train after that call. His effects were packed up and sent after him. "I had to get that man out of here before he got to my boys," the "Head" said.

GARY, ROMAIN

The more I read of Gary the (really) crazier I think he was in a
book like *Pseudo*, which is charmingly crazy. Lady I'm working
on the film with has been in France doing interviews with people who knew him. It seems he was much shrunk, and put on
various mood pills. He sounds quick-cycle bi-polar to me. They
say Jean Seberg's death made him very depressed, but *Pseudo*
seems hyper-manic to me. The frenzy of punning is hyper-
manic surely, as it was, more mildly, in Ez.

GREEK

Soon I will be fifty—and
I haven't yet learned Greek!
This calls for drastic revision
of life pattern don't you agree?
Assuming, of course, that we
don't all blow up first.

GERMANS

About the Krauts. My German friends always say there are good Germans and bad Germans. The family I boarded with in Gauting bei Muenchen to learn some German were good. He was an artist who painted postcards of village scenes, the people in my "Melody with Fugue" story. They pulled the blinds when the brownshirts were staging a march. Eva Hesse and the whole gang at Hanser Verlag are OK. But certain things I observed in German boys I skied with were not so good; there were streaks of meanness, even cruelty. And they let drop remarks that inferred Chermans were better than auslanders, more manly, more guts. Think of the Prince of Homburg before he saw some light. Could part of it be the way they're brought up as children? Ordnung und Gehorsam. Your dad or your teacher tells you to do something and you bloody well do it, pünktlich und ploetzlich.

I remember a bad scene in a train when Sara (Papagene) and I (Papageno)—we went to the opera whenever we could get Studentenkarte—were going up to Garmisch for some hiking. We put our feet up on the opposite empty seat. A fat old Kraut went off his mind with rage, tried to get the conductor to throw us off the train. What makes them that way? (Not that we don't have some terrible ethnic hatreds in the cities.) Had it anything to do with the country being divided into rival principalities? There's some of that in some of the Kleist stories. And Wagner was not such a nice chap, though he did have the redeeming feature of borrowing the housemaid's underpants—some humanity in that. As far as I know Goethe was a decent sort. And now there are the skinheads trying to run out the gipsies and the Turks. But at least the TV shows big demonstrations against them. Some of them learned something.

GIRLS

use   Ubi sunt qui ente nos in hoc mundo
      fuere

use the greet couplet from Nox mihi
cendile with or without my efficecious
for persueding girls funny

GIRLS

PERSONAL AND CONFIDENTIAL

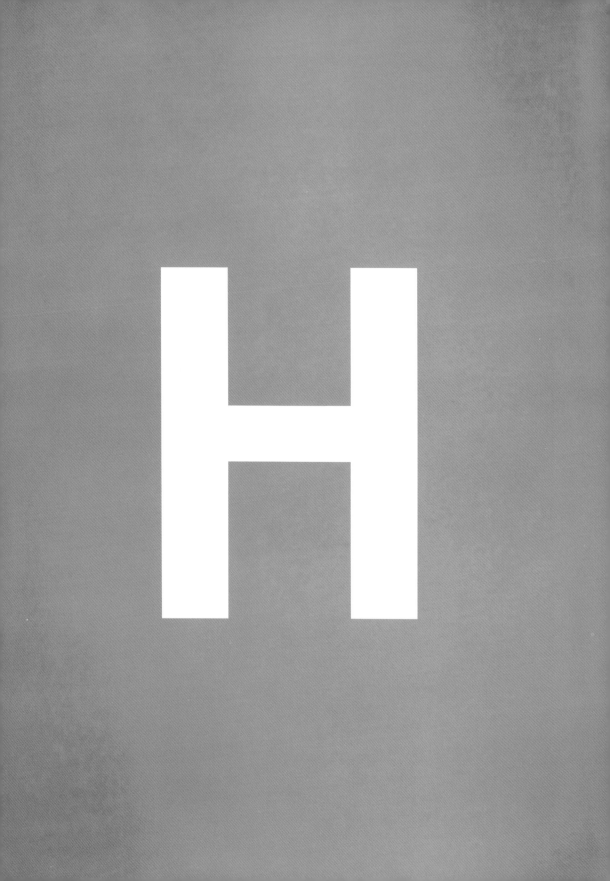

What do I first remember about my wonderful friend Jack Heinz? I remember the back of his neck.

When Jack and I first started skiing together we remembered the poverty of childhood. We grew up in great houses, but we never had any money. Money, no doubt, was corrupting for children. I had an allowance of 25¢ a week. Perhaps Jack had 50¢. It took us a long time to get over that. Once, I remember, it must have been about 1945, we bought a Monte Cristo cigar in a restaurant. It probably cost a dollar. We declined a second. Jack took out a penknife and cut it in half. We each smoked half a cigar and felt virtuous. But there was a gradual relaxation of the Presbyterian ethic. It was Jack who taught me all I know about wines and good cooking. The highpoint was our visit for lunch to M. Point's restaurant near Lyons. There were thirteen courses beginning with pâté of nightingale. Between each course the sommelier would approach with "a nice little local wine you'll enjoy." Neither of us dared to drive the car. A taxi took us to the local inn to sleep it off.

I hope I don't give the impression that Jack gave up work in the winter. The "Old Firm," as he called the company, was always in his mind. Once in Ketchum, near Sun Valley, he discovered that a restaurant was putting Hunts' ketchup (the kind that runs) into Heinz bottles. He pursued the matter in the kitchen.

Then there was the affair of the mouse in the pickle bottle from the Berkeley plant. We flew to California and Jack handled it beautifully. Two free bottles were offered for every one turned in. And when the mad employee was found, he was discharged, but given severance and not prosecuted. Jack was a kind man, a sensitive man, a forbearing man.

HEINZ

Once we were in Crespi's in Rome and there was a great spinach soup that I liked. He went out to the kitchen and tipped the chef to give him the recipe. When he got home to Pittsburgh he gave it to his chef at the plant and had him copy it. Then he had the plant turn out 1000 cans and gave batches of a hundred to me and other friends.

ALTA
1961

HAWKES, JOHN

Dear Jack,

I have now had an opportunity to read the essay on you very carefully, and I'm sorry to have to report back to you—because I had wanted very much to be enthusiastic about it—that I find it pretty dismal . . .

I find him a pretentious writer, but without much lucidity. Now, I ask you, just look at this sentence in the conclusion: "Even as Hawkes is the artificer of release for his readers in becoming the surrogate victim and victimizer of our fearful and distorted loves, so, as artist-protagonist (and the participative reader becomes artist-protagonist as well), his felt-perceptions of the absurdities of contradiction are themselves liberated into the free and joyful flow of energy." Now, goodness knows, your writing does have "a free and joyful flow of energy" to a degree which few others around us today do, and if he could just write about it in language as simple as those few words I would be more than happy, but, alas, he doesn't, and, instead, plunges us into an almost impenetrable jungle of heavy language and ponderous concepts.

Naturally you are pleased that he wrote about you, and that he obviously put so much time into studying your work, but I think, Jack, that you have got to begin to be a little bit self-protective because more and more of the critics, and young professors, are going to start writing about you, and if you take it each time as a personal kindness, and try to show some form of personal appreciation, you can get involved in some very time-consuming, and perhaps even embarrassing situations. The next stage after this will be the PhD thesis writers, and those boys, believe me, can really eat up your time, if you let them.

Today's new word was
Haecceity (2 "c"s in the
Middle), hardly a melopoeic
Word. It's quite hard to
Pronounce. But it has much
Substance because it means
Thisness (and by later usage
Here and now). It comes from
The Latin pronoun *haec*,
Which means *this*. Just remember
Hic, haec, hoc from school.
What's more substantial than
A *this*; it's closer to us
than a *that*. If you have a
This you have something you
Can grab hold of, that won't
Slip away from you, that may
Persist as long as you're
Around in the here and now

HELLMAN, LILLIAN

I met Fuentes at the both-Americas literary conference which Rodman Rockefeller put on at Chichen Itza. Fuentes was OK. That's where I met Nicanor Parra, the Chilean poet, who became a lifelong friend. But I didn't like Lillian Hellman at all: what a raspy character. When I knocked at her door to try to borrow one of her books (hoping to butter her up) she only opened the door four inches and said words to the effect: "Fuck off, you rapist." Perhaps I had interrupted her communings with the ghost of Dashiell Hammett. Alfred Knopf, my idol in publishing, knew about the Mayan pyramids and had fitted himself out at Abercrombie & Fitch with a pyramid-climbing costume: lederhosen, an insect-repellent shirt, knitted knee-length stockings, boots with rubber cleats, and a pith topee. The conference secretary filmed his ascent.

HOGG

A BOOK
OF THE
GREATEST
INUTILITY
AND ZIP

You probably know it, but if you don't, I think you'd like

The Confessions of a Justified Sinner (1824) by James Hogg

which Cresset Press reissued in 1947 with a curious, ecstatic

introduction by Gide. It is a story about the (Calvinist?)

Predestination cult in Scotland. What you do is to get your

double, who can make himself look like anybody, to kill

off people who don't agree with your theology. And this is OK,

Jesus loves it, because you are making a better world. And

all written in a delicious style of the XVIIieme, interlarded

with comic folk wisdom in Scots.

HOMOSEXUALITY

Hugh
Lesser Goldman
Ebury Street
Choate
Tennessee
Danielou

HORSES

If you'd like to read it, I can lend you Jack Hawkes's new novel.
It's called *Sweet William,* and it's written entirely by a horse.
I urged him to forget this terrible project, and curb his obses-
sion, but he didn't. I hate horses. Horses hate me. My earliest
childhood memory (age 3) was when dear Black Annie was
going to drive me in the pony cart to Lake Ole (Florida) to pad-
dle on the beach. The pony took off before I was in the cart and
my foot was run over. The persecution has continued ever since.
When I try to put the bridle on they bite me. When I try to saddle up they kick me. They bloat their stomachs so the saddle
falls off. They run me under low branches of trees. Hopeless.

HUTCHINS, MAUDE

Maude Hutchins (wife of Bob), author of the early poem-novel which the *Chicago Tribune* referred to as *The Dairy of Love,* also used slips. She would write her little [lubsierties?] on slips and put them in a Chinese pot. When the pot was full she would spread them on the rug until she had her plot and then write the book. After four of those I told her, "Maude, there are other subjects such as *War + Peace,* why don't you try that?" And we were no longer friends. But, I didn't mind because she insisted on being taken to lunch and would drink 3 martinis very slowly, while she talked away, and I would get hungrier and hungrier. (Can I tell mean stories like that in my book?)

HARVARD MAGAZINE

The writer from *Harvard Magazine* was down to pump me about my depraved life. I told him he must say that I write verse, not poesies, and that my idol is Ogden Nash, or a step up from that, Cummings.

HITLER

Today died Paul von Hindenburg, Reichspräsident and Generalfeldmarshall in his eighty-sixth year. Tonight in the Odeonsplatz we watched the black-uniformed SS brigades assemble before the Feldherrnhalle in mourning. Torches were lighted that burned late into the night, fiery and red in the night. All the bells tolled in disharmony and flags hung draped in black. Standing in the crowd we were driven slowly back by the mounted police as far as the Galeriestrasse so that a great empty space lay between civilian herd and sacred soldiery. There suddenly one plucked at my sleeve, and was my much loved tutor Dana Durand, as informal, omniscient, and clever as ever. We joined talk to beer in a café and threshed out all matters of current politic. He works daily at Medieval manuscripts in the Staatsbibliothek on the Ludwigstrasse, probing old maps as well. He told of the power and financial skullduggery of Schaact. German bonds are deflated by erroneously lowering the gold reserve and then bought in with the funds that should go for interest. The murderers of Dolfuss appear to have confessed that they expected to find Rintelen in the Chancellory, and finding him not there knew not how to pull off their coup d'etat. German papers made no mention that the job had been done by Nazis, but referred to the murderers as "people" or discontented officials. . . . Earlier in the day we played tennis in the courts of the Englische Garten. . . . Shortly after the death of Hindenburg, Der Führer either passed or had passed a law combining the offices of Reichspräsident and Chancellor in his own person. The Clean-up of June is said to have been carried out by the extremely loyal Prussian Police, who were simply given 77 names and told to dispose of the owners, the which they did with precision.

MÜNCHEN
2.8.34

HEMINGWAY

I saw Vittorini when I was in Milan about Easter time and he told me, with much emotion, of your forwarding the check to him. He was deeply touched. But also deeply embarrassed, as accepting didn't fit in with his very correct feelings and his sense, which I shared, that you had already done so much to help him get well started in USA. The way it stands now I think he plans to buy you an artwork of some kind with the money which he will give you the next time you are in Italy. But don't tell him I said so, as I believe he wants it to be a surprise.

As you doubtless heard, the book did very nicely, and I know that your introduction was a major factor in its success. It would be nice to think that virtue met its reward without exterior pushes and prods, but it just ain't so, at least not with the papers full of turds like Sterling North. Did you see his pukage on the subject? I tore it up in a rage, but I think he thought V's writing was amateurish, or schoolboyish, or some such phrase.

FINCA.VIGIA, SAN FRANCISCO DE PAULA, CUBA

2/6/50

Dear Mr. Laughlin :

Thank you for your letter   about the Vittor
book and the check . I sent the check to Vittorini
as I had   done the Introduction to help him and not to
make money . Am delighted the book had such good
reviews and hope it did well .

Do you   have a good translator , really good
from Italian   into English ? There is a boy here from
Venice who has a short story and soon will have a
novel to translate . I want to go over them with him
in English   but I cannot take the time for translation now
with page proofs   of my own book comeing next and a great
back-log of correspondence .

This boy , Gianfranco Ivancich ,(If you know
Venice you know the name) served with Rommel   when they
kicked the hell out of   us at Gafsa ,fought in the
rear guard actions , was wounded and invalided home and then
,when Italy came in on our side , served with a band of
Partisans in the north . Our heavies unloaded on the
family's country house which was very beautiful and
which I remember from when I was a boy   and after and
some phony partisans (the stick-up variety) shot his father
and threw   his body into the Tagliamento .

His material is completely authentic and I
know the whole story . I feel a great sense of shame for
many of the things we did in Italy and it is a very
small thing of contrition to try ᴛᴀxxɪᴇx to help beginning
Italian writers   in any way that I can .

So would you be good enough to let me know
about the translator and   what he or she charges . It would
be best to have the short story translated first and then
the novel .

Whoever publishes the book I would be happy
to write a preface for it as I did for Vittorini .
Scribners have asked about the book and Charley asked me
to act for him .But I have made no promises to anyone .

How is your ski-ing ? Did you see Colo at
Aspen ? Mrs. Hemingway broke her left leg this year
for a change . It was a great snow year at Cortina .
If you ever write to Salt Lake - but I don't suppose
you do and I should do it myself .

Best always ,

Ernest Hemingway .

HIRAM HANDSPRING

I'm not sure who my double really is. He began long ago when I started putting the name Hiram Handspring on comical parody pieces in the New Directions annuals. A clown, harmless fellow. But now I think he has become rather sinister. He keeps pushing me to write everything in a sort of black humour, a sardonic tone. *J'ai peur de lui. Il faut que tu me sauve de lui!* My shrink is not much help. He doesn't believe in doubles and just laughs.

At 82 H. took up literature. He was advised to darken his locks and did so.

After a study of current literary productions, H. decided that the quickest way to get ahead was to steal from successful old poets. It's poet eat poet declared Handspring.

But H.'s literary plan did not seem to work. Helen Vendler paid no attention to him and *The New Yawper* did not print him. Disillusioned, Handspring abandoned literature. He joined Douglas Fairbanks, Jr., and Errol Flynn in the Foreign Legion. When H. returned from the Foreign Legion he found a world he didn't like. It was full of structuralists and Femulists and there was a cowboy. He retired to a funny farm where he is very popular and very happy.

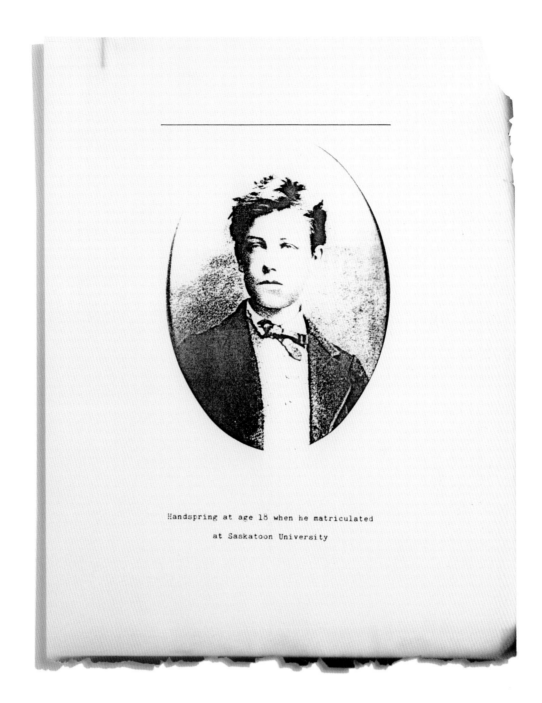

Handspring at age 18 when he matriculated
at Saskatoon University

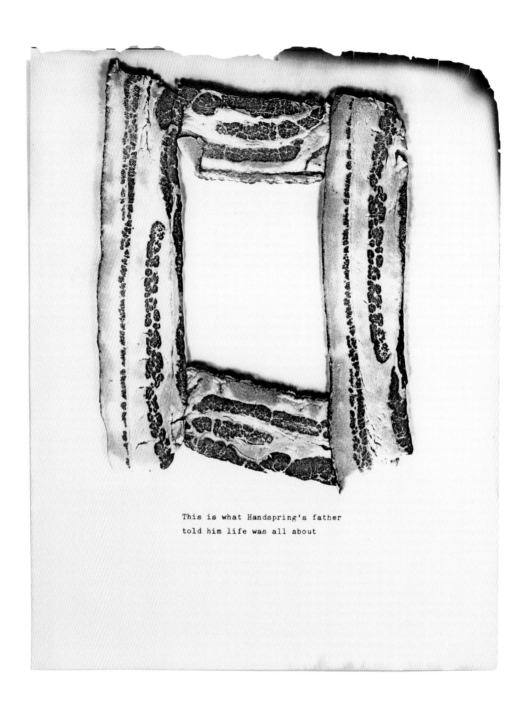

This is what Handspring's father
told him life was all about

This is what Handspring decided for
himself that life is all about ▮

IRISH

Because most of the Irish in Pittsburgh were workmen or servants there was a fiction that we were Scots. My father ordered a complete Scottish outfit for me, kilt and sash, sporran and dirk, in which I enjoyed showing off on special occasions. To be sure, the Laughlins were Protestant Irish from the Pale, which meant that they had originated in Scotland.

IRELAND

Oirrreland and the Oirrish turned out to be great, in fact wonderful. We didn't find my ancestors' graves—the grass had grown over them since 1824—but it was a Powerful Emoshunal Experience. I read Yeats while it rained and got all Schwarmey.

IRRITATING PEOPLE

I hope that all of the unpleasantness with that Chinese fellow has passed. I'm afraid I was not sufficiently supportive at that time, but he seemed like such a ridiculous monkey. I hoped that it wouldn't upset you. The world is full of a large number of irritating people.

INDIA

India began about 1919 when I was in fourth grade at Miss Simonson's School for the right children of East End Pittsburgh. It was on a map in my geography book, a pear-shaped red shape that hung out from the bottom of Asia, the largest continent.

India interested me. Vasco da Gama sailing there from Portugal. Hastings and Clive. The Mogul emperors playing chess with slaves for the chessmen. I imagined roles for myself. I was a heroic Muslim Sepoy in the Mutiny shooting British redcoats because they made me lick pork grease off my bullets. I had a nightmare about suffocating in the Black Hole of Calcutta. India became important to me but I never imagined I would get there . . .

So it wasn't until 1953 after Robert Hutchins had signed me on with the Ford Foundation that Bob's co-director of the Foundation, the brilliant and golden-tongued Milton Katz ("Uncle Miltie" as we affectionately called him) sent me out to India. My mission was to investigate the state of Indian book publishing, which was said to be deplorable. The Foundation already had a strong agricultural program going under Douglas Ensminger; this was to be its first look at a cultural project. I was hardly an authority on publishing; my New Directions effort had always been small potatoes and limited to highbrow books. But I was handy and eager to get to India; they took a chance on me. If the selection had happened a few years later, when the Foundation office had been moved to New York and its procedures highly organized, when it became a bureaucracy, I wouldn't have had such good luck. But in the early days when the Foundation was setting up shop in a private house in Pasadena—some wag, probably Hutchins, had put up a sign on the lawn: ITCHING PALMS—everything was very casual and off-the-cuff.

INDIA

It's hot here now and I imagine I'm back in India. In Delhi I would arise at 4 to go play golf with Khushwant Singh, the historian of the Sikhs, on the course where the beautiful ruins of the Mughul temples are. Such a nice man. He would let me watch him wind his long hair and then his turban, a different color for each day. Lawnmowers had not yet arrived in Delhi. There would be hundreds of women crouched on the course, pulling grass with their fingers. If there was an appointment it would be at nine. Then the heat closed down and everyone took it easy. In the hotel there was a punkah-wallah who would pull an overhead cloth for a fan. One of mine would lie on his back and pull the fan-string with his big toe. Life would renew about six. That's when people socialized and paid calls. Many people called on me, thinking they would get money from the Ford Foundation, but they didn't. Indian peasants, out in the fields, work like crazy, turning the tread wheels that raise water from the wells to the irrigation ditches. Better class (or caste) Indians work as little as possible. The most beautiful sights in plains country are the sunsets. At that time the peasants are burning cow patties to heat water for their suppers. The dark smoke rises and joins into the sunset orange. The smell of the smoke is lovely, a very subtle fragrance, like no flower. They say it is aphrodisiacal.

INDIA

Have I told you of dinners at Sir Jehangir & Lady Jeejeeboy's in
Bombay? The grandfather of this elegant Parsee had been given
the name Jeejeeboy because he took care of the Maharajah of
Gujurat's "jee-jees." I forget how the money had been made but
there was a lot of it. The dinner table seated twenty and behind
each chair there was a servitor in silken dhoti and red turban,
but with bare feet (to be more soundless). There was a complete
Maharastrian dinner and a complete French one from which one
could choose. The best cooks in Bombay were all from Goa.
In the house of Sir Benegal and Lady Rama Rau, where I visited
for a time, the major domo told me with pride that "his" chef
could cook for six months without duplication of menu. For the
dinners at Naroji Castle, the Jeejeeboy's place, Rolls were sent to
the dwellings or hotels of the guests to fetch and return them.
And the J's would have been, in accordance with their religion,
exposed on the Tower of Silence to be gobbled by crows and
fierce hawks. Death a great leveler.

In Trivandarum the Maharajah had us to tea in his palace garden.
Very handsome. He is an innocuous young man with not much
future as his state has been absorbed into India. All he has left to
do now is to be the religious leader of the region. So he goes to the
temple every morning. Spoke a lovely Oxford English but had his
forehead copiously smeared with yellow paint—caste marks. He
has a fortune of several hundred millions Rupees but the govt will
take it away in Inheritance Taxes when he dies.

I sat at tea with his Mother-in-law—the Maharanee—who
reminded me of Hattie, Aunt Leila's cook. Looked and talked
exactly like her, though more of an English accent. She was very

JL TO FAMILY
1953

nice and told me long stories out of Hindu mythology. I have found this the most successful conversational gambit with all Hindus. It's often hard to talk to them but the minute you ask them "Who was Parvati?" or "Who was Bali Vijayan?" They launch into the legends and tell them with a great deal of sense of humor. It is all a vital part of their lives. They learn these stories as children and never seem to grow out of them.

When Joyce opened the
door for me in Paris he said:
"I think, Mister Logulan,
we met for the larst toime
on the battlefield of Clontarff."
Then he explained that my
name meant "Danish pirate."

Kenner is to speak at Brown on April 28th. I assume it will be a public lecture. Do you want me to see if Jack can get you and Walter invited down? They told me at Princeton where I blubbered last week, that his new lecture on *Dubliners* is very interesting, that he proves that JJ's stories are full of stuff from the Bible. This I want to hear. I didn't know Kaffliks were allowed to read the Good Book.

I never saw the real JJ because
I never went drinking with him.

JL'S GREAT AMERICAN NOVEL

. . . on the battered little Corona. I was still trying to write the Greet American Novel. It was about dreary, Philistine Pittsburgh and how an angry young man busts loose "to forge in the smithy of his soul the uncreated conscience of his race" (Joyce). What did I really understand about Pittsburgh that I was trying so hard to escape? I knew that Andy Mellon was a mean old man; he wouldn't let us kids swim in his swimming pool across Woodland Road. Things like that . . . but I also remember the mores of some contemporaries of my class. They drove too fast, drank too much, and even fornicated in the golf course sand traps of the Allegheny Country Club. How to put the pieces together? The Great American Novel will always be *Moby Dick*.

JEWS

But the recollections at the Poetry Center in Chicago went over. Largely, if you will forgive me, because there were quite a few very cultivated Jewish people in the audience, art patron types. I had them in my palm in 3 minutes and played on them like a fiddle. Ann's mother always said:

Never settle in a city
where there aren't Jews:
the food will be terrible
and there'll be no culture.

JARRELL, RANDALL

Randall Jarrell referred to
me as "Goody Two-Shoes."

JAPAN

Here around Kyoto, the old capital, which sits in a bowl of wooded hills, they have some beautiful little temple shrines in groves, all beautifully kept and as peaceful and lovely. At one of them we were given ceremonial tea—green stuff, quite thick & frothy—and sat on the matting by the open side for a long time looking out at the wonderful landscape of wooded hills. I wish I could spend more time up here. But must go back to work. It is difficult work because the people are so different. You have to fuss around a lot to get an answer out of them. The first time you see them they protest that they are not good enough to write what you want and send you to some friend who is better. Then the friend sends you back to the first man who is, he says, the only one who can do the job. And they won't say when they can finish the work, nor will they discuss the fee. It is all very complicated. It would be an amusing game except that I have so little time & want to get things lined up so that I can leave. But they are rather sweet with all their pretty manners.

KNOPF

I did know old Alfred Knopf very well . . . He published so many good books over his lifetime and when the Ford Foundation set me up at Intercultural, he kindly came on my Board and was most helpful in deflating the pomposity of other members.

KLEIST

And what did Kleist say to Henrietta Vogel in the last moments before he shot her on the bank of the WannSee? The kind of thing I brood about. Goethe was enough older than Kleist so it might have been some poignant lines from *Werther*.

KIRSTEIN, LINCOLN

A great man (also homosexual, as I first discovered when Spender's French lover, Count Anne de Bieville (a man), invited me to his apartment in Paris and there was Tchelitchew's enormous portrait of Lincoln, entirely naked except for menacing boxing gloves on his hands, and LK in a boxer's pose).

Also re LK must deal with publishing his remarkable book of poems *Rhymes of a PFC* (of which the army bought 750 copies, not exactly realizing what was in it).

And must try to dig out somehow whether it was LK or TS Eliot who told me when I joined up with the Ford Foundation: "What are you trying to do, become Ambassador to China?"

KEROUAC, JACK

Dear Mr Laughlin I'm very glad you were pleased by our surprise visit, which I thought might have deterred you from doing your work. I wrote to Prof. Pearsall for the schizophrenic writings, a wonderful idea for a real true pure anthology. Also, will use all your Anemone poems you marked. I write intros to each author, and my intro to you will be that you are "beat" because you took more chances than any other publisher. (as Jonathan Williams also claims). Rec'd the CODY ms. and am fixing it and will bring it into New Directions office 6th aveneu on afternoon of May 29th (Friday) ready for printer. I am removing various items like "Rusty's" hometown which was really "Lusk," you were wise to send it back. Calling her "Josephine". Incidentally, I NEVER submit manuscripts to publishers with ONE typo, so that explains some of your queries. As to funny misspellings, as you say sometimes they're charming. Everything coming along.

Jack Kerouac

Dear Jack—

Many thanks for your card, and it certainly is wonderful   5.25.59

to think that I may end up in a book along with the Beats . . .

KARR, MARY

It was a mistake to make the trip up to Cambridge for the poetry reading on Brattle Street. The 3-hour car trip was a penance. But it was a benefit for *Ploughshares*, a most worthy magazine. Donald Hall is one of its floating editors, but he wasn't there, he has cancer. Rotten luck, such a good man. He was wonderful to Ezra helping him to get the Cantos in shape that went into the *Paris Review* interview when Ez was so muddled in his head. A rough evening my head was banging so. The Texas kid, Mary Karr, got me through the dinner before the reading. She sat beside me and kept squeezing my hand under the table. A dear, dandy, small but vast-souled girl. (Pretty legs, too, but I was way past that.) Did I send you her book of poems ND just published, *Devil's Tour*? Let me know if you want it. Pretty good stuff: post-culturally dense and nice noises. So I wouldn't have to make table talk to strangers, always hard for me, she gave me a steady stream of the history of her life, worthy of Aubrey.

She grew up in a family in Port Arthur, Tex, who were all manic-depressives, really wild ones. She couldn't stand them. She saved up $100 from baby-sitting and, at fifteen, took off hitching for California. There her Samaritan was a surfer at one of the beaches. They found a wrecked car, parked it at the beach, and lived in it for many months, she earning her bread with odd jobs but a noble, clean-hearted girl (she says) turning no tricks. VERY bright and ambitious. She wangled herself a full scholarship at Pomona College. Did well, graduated, won a scholarship for a masters at Harvard in English. Eager to prosper, she got a scholarship at the B. School.

Then real money came along in the form of a nice young man from Old Westbury, Long Island—his pappa is the lawyer for the Whitney family. That didn't last too long as she didn't fit in at Meadowbrook Club polo. They split and she got a job teaching English at Syracuse. Seems to have read most everything.

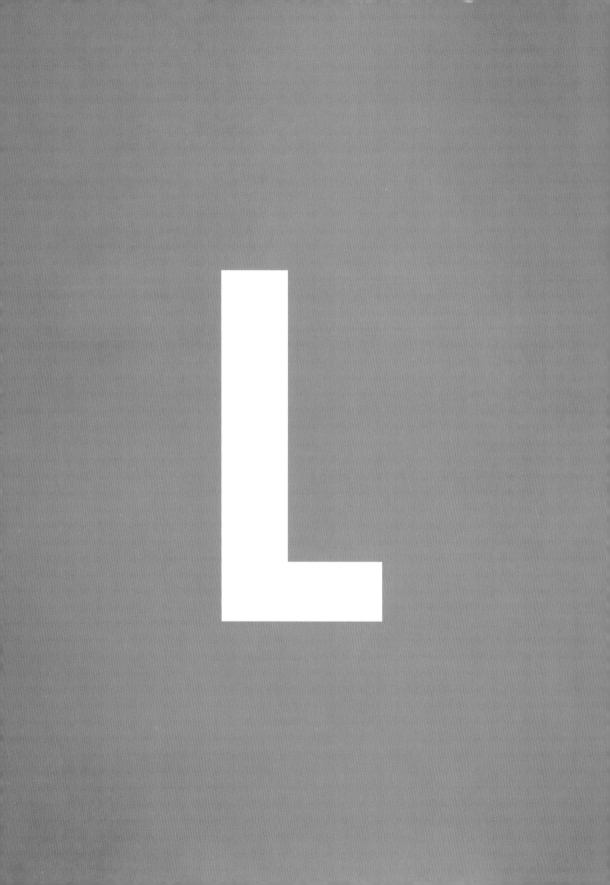

LEWIS, WYNDHAM

Wyndham Lewis: "Why don't you stop New Directions, your books are crap."

LOVE

Cicero noted that an old love pinches like a crab.

LAUGHLINS

. . . Uncle Roger assembled 7863 specimens of the eggs of birds. RIP. His work is done. In fact if you wanted me to go draymatic and do a Buddenbrooks I could write:

JAMES I COLLECTED BIBLES
    " II "   DOLLARS
    " III "   BLONDES
    " IV "   REJECTION SLIPS

Journey to the End of The Readers' Patience

LEVERTOV, DENISE

Denise has indeed fluffied up her hair. I wonder whether she does it with curling irons or goes to the hair parlor. Her most lovable feature, not that I would ever tell her so, is the space between two of her front upper teeth. Dormesson, who is not an entirely reliable witness, reports that this fissure drove the poet Guillevic mad with insatiable passion.

Hmmm. I hope I don't speak disrespectfully of Denise; I love and revere her. But she frequently disapproves of me. I tried to fix it up with Alice Quinn, the poetry editor at the *New Yorker*, that Alice would ask her for an occasional poem. For reasons that I can't follow this was taken as an insult, that she would publish in such a place (even though they pay big money). . . . My early crime was that at Harvard I read a saucy poem about "Girls Legs," for me a tender subject. Denise snatched the page and burned it on the steps of Houghton. I'll never live that down. But it's wonderful in these times that someone has high principles and defends them so strongly.

My admiration for her continually increases. One of the things I liked most about her is her social commitment. I haven't counted the times she has gone to jail for her beliefs. Most publicized perhaps was the time she lay down on the sidewalk in front of the Nuclear Regulatory Commission in Washington until she was carted off in the paddy wagon. I don't know that she has actually scaled the fence of the nuclear power plant in New Hampshire but I'm sure she gave it a good try. This passion and courage comes through in her work. Some people object to what her politics do to her "social" poems. Her second English publisher, Tom Maschler at Cape, refused her book containing the Berkeley riot poems. He found it too political. I thought this was odd for a man who was making two trips a year to Havana.

Another charming thing happened when they had me do a poetry reading at Harvard, and Harry Levin was in the audience, and we came to my poem that is entitled "Ars Gratia Artes," and I hollered over to Harry, "is that a tag from Horace?" and he briefly replied, "No, from Metro-Goldwyn-Mayer." He is so learned, he even knew the name of the Frenchman who had invented the phrase from whom MGM got it.

The Harvard Classical Club

presents the

PHILOCTETES

OF

SOPHOCLES

Harry Levin, over the years the closest of my Harvard faculty friends, was still a non-teaching Junior Fellow when I was in college. My first recognition of his astounding mental powers came when the Classics Department put on Sophocles' *Philoctetes*, in Greek, in the Lowell House common room. Robert Fitzgerald, already an accomplished classicist, took the lead. The other big part in the play is that of Neoptolemus, son of Achillies, who went with Odysseus to Lemnos to persuade Philoctetes, to whom Hercules had given his magic bow, to join the siege of Troy. The director was Milman Parry, the famous scholar who showed the survival of the Homeric epic in the contemporary oral poetry of Yugoslavia. A few days before the performance Neoptolemus fell ill. Parry had no understudy. But he had heard of Harry Levin's fabulous memory. The story goes that Parry locked Levin in his study and taught him the whole long part phonetically. None of us who watched the play suspected that Harry was not a practiced Greek student. He was word and accent perfect.

MISS LOEB LIBRARY

We would not strengthen our faculties if we didn't construe.
We couldn't get the true feel of the language if we didn't go
word to word to see how they were put together. At worst, we
would not develop *character* through such indolence. My first
years I shunned the Loeb unless I got in a jam. But with the
book publishing to handle I saw I would never get the reading
for my exams done without [the Loeb]. The bookstores in
Harvard Square referred me to the Harvard University Press,
the American distributors of the series, for what I needed.
When I entered the atrium of the press I was astounded to
behold at the desk, lucent and lambent, though chewing the
eraser of her pencil, the Virgin Goddess of learning herself,
Pallas Athena.

It was a vision, but she was real. No doubt it was she. Her
copper colored hair was arranged like a helmet over her head.

LISH, GORDON

Dear Rain King,

Est – ce qu'il pleut aussi dans ton coeur? Be I your sponge to dry your tears.

But I wish you had been here this morning. It might have been the turning point in your evil life. There was a kock (oh, sorry, what an awful Freudianism) I mean knock and I opened to Jesus. It was the Bible lady from the Jehovah's Witnesses and her idiot 14-year-old son who was slobbering delicately from the corners of his mouf. She had come to "share the scriptures" with me. As she was quite nice looking I invited her in, though hoping that the monster would not spot the rug. She asked me to get my Bible (fortunately we always keep one in the guest room) and we read passages of her designation for nearly an hour. She said I read just beautifully and had I ever felt I had a calling. Mostly we read from Revelations, because there everything is explained about the Atom Bomb and such matters. She really wasn't bad. It was hard for me to keep my eyes on God's word and not scan her nice gambs. Suddenly her offspring spoke up and declared that the proof of the complete truth of the Bible was that it was exactly the same in the Dead Sea Scrolls. He said teach at school had talked about the Dead Sea Scrolls. You believe in the Devil, in Satan, don't you? Yes, I said, I know him personally, he has an office on 50th St in New York. Any day I'm going to cast him out of himself. Also, I said, I've read about him in Milton's Paradise Lost. *She got a vague look on that. Then she asked me to avow that the Good Book is absolute and complete truth. I thought it might be nice to kneel close beside her and take the vow. But I thought better of it. The monster had large feet in heavy boots and might have kicked my teeth out. I weazled out of that by talking about myths. She wasn't sure what a myth was so I read her the definition in Webster. Fortunately Webster says, among*

other things, that a myth can be the vehicle for religious truth.
That cheered her up some. A myth, I told her, helps people to
remember God's great truths. She seemed to buy that. To my
surprise, she insisted that there was no such place as Hell, but
was vehement, quoting various passages, about how God is
going to destroy evil-doers. AND THAT MEANS YOU, LISH.
I think she would have liked to stay all day, but I didn't see
any percentage in it with the monster around. But she
said she would return.

    If she gives advance notice I'll try to get you up here. She sold
me for 75 cents a splendid little volume called "The Truth that
Leads to Eternal Life." I read this while watching my team, the
Steelers, cream the Jets, and it is full of verity & knowledge. Shall
I purchase a copy for you to keep in your desk drawer? You could
slip it out and glance at a page in moments of turpitude and
temptation. I think you would particularly profit from these
chapters: "Why Has God Permitted Wickedness Until Our Day?",
"The Reason Why a Little Flock Goes to Heaven", "The Last
Days of the Wicked System of Things."

    Beloved Brother, I truly want to help you. I don't want my
pleasant days above to be disturbed by your piteous cries of pain
from Down There. Don't laugh, Brother, the Bible tells me so.
Now don't be petulant about Mr. 0. For a sophisticated man, you
have little insight. Don't you realize that he does as he does
because his peter is small. At least, I guess so. We do not demand
inspection before hiring. News Flash: I have metempsychosed into
Desiderius Erasmus of Rotterdam. Proof of this will reach you
when I get it typed out. Ways of keeping from doing serious work
for AAK. GET DOWN ON YOUR KNOBBLY OLD KNEES
AND PRAY BEFORE IT IS TOO LATE.

LOVE

Our village love counselor tells her lovelorn young clients that kittens can't be caught but if you stay where you are and do something interesting the kitten will soon come to you.

LOWELL, AMY

. . . I made my worst gaffe. I asked about his notorious sister Amy, the cigar-smoking poet of Imagism. About her he wanted to say nothing at all. I did not make a good impression. When the next day Parthenia telephoned to thank him for the dinner, he asked her, "Parthenia, why must you always fall in love with worthless men?" She thought this was amusing. I am not thick-skinned and was hurt and offended by it. Resentful. So it was with a certain pleasure that I learned later at a dinner in Lowell's honor at Lowell House each guest when he picked up his napkin found a picture of Sacco and Vanzetti hidden under it. (Lowell, of course, had been a member of the commission appointed by the Governor of Massachusetts to review the death sentence handed out by the courts to the fishmonger and the cobbler. Their decision was a foregone conclusion. The men were dangerous anarchists.)

LEWIS, WYNDHAM

I think it would be very tiring to be a taxi driver. Wyndham Lewis, they say, used to ride in taxis in London in order to get literary opinions. I don't believe this story. Wyndham was an extremely nasty man. He dumped one of his girls who had three children by him without giving her a penny.

LOWELL, CAL

Things to remember to do on Cal Lowell.

My major contribution to him was to get him to read Williams when he came to Harvard.

Try to pin a date on my memory of Eliot's taking Cal and myself to lunch at the old Brevoort Hotel (or was it the Lafayette?) with Djuna Barnes. (Probably the Lafayette, as I see marble-topped tables.) Blank on what was discussed.

Pin down date and place of a memorial meeting for Pound when Cal read the Kung Canto so beautifully. Or did he do this in a television film? Was this the same event when Selden Rodman attacked Pound rather brutally.

Re the above: I have a dreamlike memory, rather like a frustration dream of rushing up a NYC avenue with Cal in the night, we had sat too long at dinner and couldn't find a taxi, to get to some reading on time. Some meeting or another.

Would hypnosis jog my bad memory?
Much done in TV dramas.

LUSTIG

I well remember my first contact with the work of Alvin Lustig. It must have been in 1939, when he would have been about twenty-four. It was in Los Angeles, or, rather, in one of those sugar candy suburbs that line the boulevards running toward the sea. A writer friend had told me that I ought to investigate a young chap who was doing "queer things" with type. And so I tracked him down, to a workroom in the back of a drugstore.

It took me only a few minutes to realize that I had made the acquaintance of a "person," as the saying is. The slightly-built young man with his graceful but definitely masculine movements, with those magnetic and searching eyes, had the un-shy quietness of speech and gesture which is sometimes the outward mark of inner power.

PUBLISHERS
WEEKLY
11.5.49

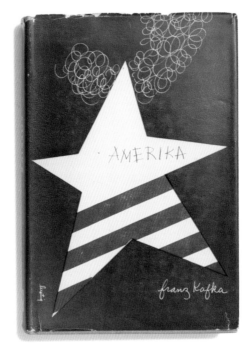

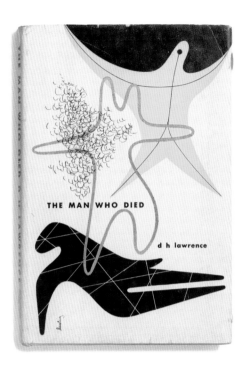

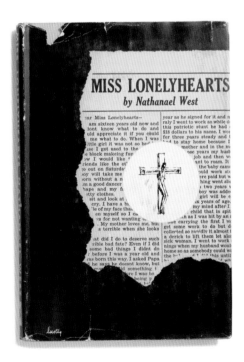

MONROE, MARILYN

This seems to be the year for digging ponds. John Morgan is making an enormous one at the head of Roaring Brook up Mountain Road, Jim Lawrence is digging one across the road not far from your house, and we have dug two in the marsh by the Mountain Road/Golf Drive corner. This last operation is known as "keeping up with the Pierces." They had dug one pond last year across Golf Drive, so we, of course, had to dig two, but we have cleaned out that very ugly swamp that was there, and I hope to be able to grow some fish in there, with a bit of luck. They were done in very quick time with a drag line, operated by a wonderful old, salty New England character, the high point of whose career was the construction of a pond in the shape of a heart for Marilyn Monroe, when she was married to Arthur Miller down near New Milford. Of this he carries a color photograph in his breast pocket. He recounts that she was "the loveliest little lady I ever met," and had him into the house for a drink every evening, it is consoling, I think, to know that goddesses still descend from Parnassus to touch with ineffable radiance the lives of humble (but worthy) mortals. Chester Dwy, for such is the honest fellow's name, still bears in his smile some trace of the apparition.

MARKETING

I think it's most important to get the "troubadours" into the title. That's a "buy me" word.

MILLER, HENRY

"I also made up with my arch-enemy, James Laughlin, of New Directions. He made a profuse and profound apology to me in the presence of several people for all he had done to thwart me. Confessed everything. Alors, nothing to do but shake hands and start all over again. Now he can't do enough for me. Gives me fifty copies free of every book he publishes of mine—for my friends."

MILLER TO
LAWRENCE
DURRELL
5.5.44

"I've made it clear to Curtis Brown that I don't give a milk shake for Laughlin that shyster impressario of bad work."

DURRELL
TO MILLER
10.1945

I wager that half the exploits in Henry Miller's *Tropics* book were imaginary. He was not Errol Flynn. He resembled the clerk in our rural general store and was equally loquacious.

MAN RAY

I haven't figured out the Man Ray. But as my old chum, that great thinker A. MacLeish remarked, "A pitcher should not mean but be." Good old Archie, was he at Harvard when you were there? A smooth apple, but sincerely smooth. My son Paul, the one who collects photographs, says that Man Ray often didn't use a camera, he had ways of exposing photographic paper to light and objects directly so that they registered. Had you heard that? The blade could be a shape that cuts off the light? As best I recall, when he shot me he did it with his Brownie, no tricks. But when he developed my face he somehow got a very soft, smooth skin texture, a baby's bottom, not my baccy-chawin' mascurlinity. Artistic.

I got to know Man and Julie well that year (about 1939) when I was living in Westwood. Such very nice People. Hospitable to a young wanderer. Man did a portrait of me in which I look very tender, soul dripping out of my eyes. Later on, when they had moved back to Paris, I'd always take them to dinner there. The best of the Surrealist Painters, maybe? That one of the Marquis de Sade made out of cement blocks. And many other good ones. One of Julie's friends was a little equestrienne.

She did fancy riding on horses in small itinerant circuses. We drifted together. She was hungry and I was young. It grieves me that I can't remember her name. But I can see her face and her small, muscular body so clearly. I wonder whatever became of her . . .

As I recount these tawdry tales of maidens deflowered and abandoned I'm reminded that Tacitus tells us that the first German gnome was, "women must weep and men remember." How true.

MY WORK DAY

"Ah thet ko nyan sourt thee
 Ok sa ko kan sourt thee."

"One's life depends on one's intelligence,
 One's fortune depends on one's karma."

Got that one from Daw Mya Sein. She says that her father used to tell the children that the last line was not an invitation to idleness, that if they did not have "nyan" (intelligence and knowledge) and "wiriya" (perseverance) they wouldn't be able to take advantage of the luck of their "ka" (karma). How true!

My days are much more leisurely. I awake at 10:27 (internal clock) having usually worked the night before till 1:30. Then I open the mail and answer by hand whatever can't wait to be dictated and sent to the office. Then work on my investments and pay the bills or pre-sort the filing for Ann O'Connor, the town clerk, who comes once a week to file systematically. Letters run about 15 a day. After lunch I read a manuscript and then play golf or go fishing, but the water is so low now in the Hollenbeck that most of the trout have fled down to better water in the Housatonic. After sports I go at a manuscript again or handle any afternoon mail. At 5:30 I have a vodka and tonic. Dr Nichols says a reasonable amount of alky is good for the ancient. After supper, I play a record or two and read the Times. Then I have my hour of "classical reading." If there is anything literary on the tube I look at it. We are lucky, we can get 3 different educational stations here. Then I start dictating answers to the letters Barry will type in the office. If I finish that before 1:30 I read manuscripts again, though, actually now, I am working more on notes for my Brown lectures than on manuscripts. They will just have to pile up till I feel fairly ready for my teaching. I guess it sounds like a pretty quiet life, but it's a relief after the early days of ND when there were three crises every day.

MacLEISH

Your lecture was the best I have heard since about 1945 when Archie MacLeish, who was trained as a lawyer, did Yeats as if he were arguing his case before the Supreme Court.

MONEY

But a lot of publishing companies were started by people who had money from one source or another. And they soon went on to diet books or cookbooks or whatever. I find it extraordinary that you have never published a book deliberately to make money.

WEINBERGER

Well, there is no objection to making money. (laughter) But it's a fact that the behemoths of conglomerate publishing aren't going to do much serious literature, though occasionally they do.

LAUGHLIN

Going deeper, is it right for banks to create money and then charge interest on it? Doesn't the Constitution say that the state should create the "coinage"? I got these subversive ideas from Ezra Pound's *ABC of Economics.* (I studied with him one year when I was bored with Harvard.) I assume that the ABC is on your office shelf for ready reference. Poor old Ezra was crackers (he mixed Social Credit with Silvio Gesell's schwungeld: paste a penny stamp on the back of the bill every month to keep it good and make it circulate). Gesell, as you know, was Minister of Finance for a week in the revolutionary government of Bavaria. Ezra was nutty but he had horse sense about debt, public, private or now credit card.

Next I'll tell about how Papa, armed with a check for 100,000 crackers, took me across Harvard Square to that old brokerage that is gone now, showed me how to study the yellow sheets and got me started with a list of "sound" blue chips: Anaconda, Columbia G & E, Du Pont, GE, National Biscuit, Penna RR (there was a Pullman car on the night train from Pittsburgh to NYC named for my great-grandfather), Standard Oil (now Exxon) and United Aircraft. Three of these I still have, enlarged by many splits.

And next I'll have a page about Mr. Ling (I'm sure you've read the book about him) who took over J & L. This little Napoleon had to have a steel company. J & L was the easiest to get because so much of the stock of both families was in trusts in banks; trust officers must accept juicy offers. Mr Ling borrowed Eurodollars and paid us $80 for the stock that was selling at $40. No regrets; he saved us from the debacle of the industry. I put most of the money into my favorite modern painters.

Then I will tell how, without ever so intending, I made a nice little packet on the Harpers takeover of J B Lippincott. In those days New Directions books were distributed by Lippincott. I was enormously honored when JBL made me a director. I noticed that their stock was selling at only 4, but I knew what the book value was. Simply because I liked the Lippincotts and wanted to show it, I bought some stock each month and followed it down to 1 1/2. The troubles for JBL began with an accident. Somebody got into the computer room and pressed a wrong button. A whole year's billings were erased. For months they had twenty girls trying to reconstruct the records from invoices. Many stores claimed mistakes and refused to pay. It was so sad. That great old firm into the ashbin.

MOTHER

*My mother didn't talk to me a great deal unless she was
planning a paddywhacking for some misdeed. I was raised
chiefly by nurses and governesses. But at least they gave
me a lot of attention.*

   *I think I told you that my mother collapsed into death
in three days and had been playing golf right up to the end.
Very obliging of her but it's not something to joke about.
And she had Jesus waiting to unlatch the great door for her.*

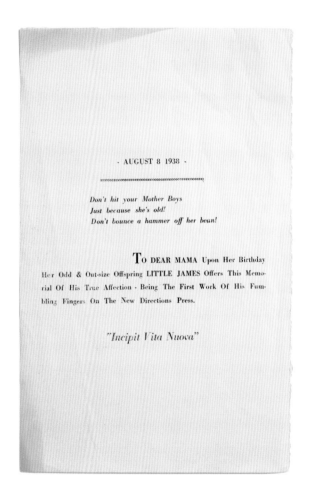

MICHAUX

SEMIOTICS

*Your piece on Michaux is another whangdoodler. Wow!
You explain it all. But I always revert to my old ways, of course.
The biographical approach. What was caused in his writing
when his beautiful wife got too near the electric heater, set her
peignoir afire, and burned to death? She was a handsome piece.
What did that signify?*

MISHIMA

He was such a charmer. Mishima I remember as a shining face
and beautiful manners. I never could understand the way he did
himself in, he seemed so Westernized. He and Bob MacGregor
were great buddies. He usually stayed with Bob when he came
to this country.

MacGREGOR, ROBERT MERCER

ND bumbles along, MacGregor is a saint mounted upon a tireless charger. I do not merit such a good man.

I repeat Bob WAS ND, but so discreet few knew it. A great publisher in every way.

MANIC DEPRESSION

Then I was fascinated to learn that she was a depressive and, I gather, bi-polar. I'm the fourth generation in the male line of manic-depressive Laughlins. And my son Robert killed himself with a kitchen knife when he couldn't take it any more at 22. With me it came on in my mid-fifties. Most of the pills in her poem I've been on. Nardil made me sick, and Prozac shot me through the roof. Now the combination of Lithium and Etrafon keeps me on fairly decent even keel. A nuisance. But I'm so blessed over my father. In the sanitaria they would put him in a tub of cold water and lace him in with canvas so he couldn't get out. I witnessed that on visits. And, as I guess you did, I saw Ezra when he was down. The famous "silence." It used to take Olga till noon on bad days to get him out of bed, make him eat, and get him dressed.

MELLON, PAUL

Speaking of races, did you see that my childhood neighbor Paul Mellon, at 85, finally won his first Derby? A fine, enormously benevolent man. Earlier in life he was very unhappy because he was so rich (the bank, Gulf Oil Co, Alcoa, Koppers, Penna RR, you name it). He went to Zurich to consult Jung about his misery. Jung told him: "Mr. Mellon, if instead of coming from the Dolder Grand in a limousine you came on the tram car, you'd feel a lot better." He did and he did. And in honor of that good advice there was the Bollingen Foundation.

MARIA

The next day Maria did not like my Pittsburgh tie. "Darling, you can't go to Passeto's in that tie. I'll get you a decent one." I did not accompany her into the Via Condotti, which debousches from the Spanish Steps, because I knew we would pass Bulgari's, where rings costing up to Lire 20,000,000 are displayed in the vitrine.

Maria returned with not one, but eight glorious cravattes. I did a rapid calculation. At that rate, my modest fortune would be exhausted in 12 years. "Darling," I said, "these are the most beautiful ties I will ever have sported, but I must check out our engagement with my mother and my Aunt Leila. I owe them that, they raised me." Aunt Leila took Maria to tea at the Colony and was charmed by her. But my mother would have none of it.

"Jamesie! A RUSSIAN! Can't you find a nice American girl who knows our ways?" I explained that Maria was not a Communist Russian; she was a white Russian, from a good if minor family in the Ukraine. I recounted the sad story of how they had to flee the motherland with only the pearls they could conceal in their bodices after the brutal assassination of the Czar and his entire family. My mother was adamant. "Remember how your cousin Gwendolyn married that French count, who spent all her money and then abandoned her. I will not permit you to marry a Russian." So Maria and I did not wed.

When Maria informed him of our "engagement" and had her mother announce it in the London *Times,* (a dear little lady whom I venerated, not only for her fine translations of Chekov's plays but for her having once called me "un chevalier sans peur et sans reproche"), Tennessee cabled Maria:

Dearest Maria and Jay your letter made me cry with happiness for you both something bright and beautiful in a dark time of course I will come and hold the crown or only to hear the music all my love and delight Tennessee

After all, marriages in these spheres are comparable to royal marriages in old Europe. And you know how they were made. Princesses royal were lined up like criminals under a hot spot and they stood there and sweated and smiled and smiled and smiled. Personally I can't imagine how they endured it, but it seemed to come with the trade, and they did, they endured it, and sometimes it must have worked out fairly well in the end.

The bubble really burst when Henry Miller gave us a delicious burlesque called "Glittering Pie." Apart from his other gifts, Henry was a wonderful comic writer. His motto was "always merry and bright." Through it all—years of constant poverty, censorship and critical neglect—he was "merry and bright." "Glittering Pie" is in the form of a letter to his pal Alfie Perles (the Mr. Corles of Pound's Canto XXXV) in Paris, in which he satirizes the culture of California where he was then living:

"At the burlesk Sunday afternoon I heard Gypsy Rose Lee sing 'Give Me a Lei.' She had a Hawaiian lei in her hand and she was telling how it felt to get a good lei, how even her mother would be grateful for a lei once in a while. She said she'd take a lei on the piano, or on the floor. An old-fashioned lei, too, if needs be . . ."

By present standards that is pretty tame stuff; it might run in the *Atlantic*. But in 1935 it was too much for Boston. In the Square the *Advocate* was selling as it never had before. Then we were raided by the Cambridge constabulary who carried off all our copies. Next day a young district attorney, who was running for re-election, went on the air to denounce sex and sin at Harvard. There followed such headlines in the Boston papers as *Decadence at Harvard* and *Sex in Mt. Auburn Street*. University Hall was as blessedly tranquil as ever; "It is not our policy to supervise or censor student publications," the Dean told the reporters. We were besieged with visitors from certain shops near Scollay Square who wanted to buy copies—and we had none to sell. In the end the district attorney was pacified with two tickets on the 50-yard line for the Yale game and there was no indictment. But the *Advocate's* graduate trustees were upset and requested that there be no more outside contributions.

MERTON, THOMAS

Tom could talk with any kind of person. He could have talked with an Eskimo.

Dear Laughlin,

*Thanks for the catalogue—you have a fine list there, I think.
Our library could certainly use the Kenyon book on Hopkins
when it comes out, & I myself think it would help the poems
along if I read Dylan Thomas' "New Poems"—unless there
is definitely something in them that is none of our
business—e.g. witchcraft. . . .*

   *The Advent (Dec. 1 to Christmas) & Lent we cannot receive
mail or answer it: but if there is proof to be read, mark "urgent"
all over it, & it will be O.K.*

MERTON, THOMAS

I loved to go down to Gethsemani to visit him at the monastery because, very simply, we had such good times. I would pick up a car at the Louisville Airport and drive down to the monastery. "Pax Intrantibus" (Peace to those who enter), it says over the gate. Father Abbot always gave Tom permission to go off with me for the day. Tom would start out circumspectly—he would go to the storage room for an old bishop's suit and exit from the monastery looking very ecclesiastical, so as not to shock the gate brother. A few miles, and he'd say "Stop here." He would go into the woods, take off his bishop's suit, put on his blue jeans, his old sweater, and his beret, and get back into the car with a sigh of relief. Then we would head east, stopping I mustconfess, at a few rural beer parlors along the way; Tom was always very popular with the local farmers. He knew how to talk to all kinds of people—they found him funny and they liked him.

I'll never forget my first trip to Gethsemani It was after New Directions had published *Thirty Poems*. Tom and I had corresponded, talking about other books that he might write, and the abbot invited me to visit him. This was a very novel experience for me, going to stay in a monastery—which, if I accepted the prejudices of my Presbyterian mother, I would have considered an invention of the devil himself.

Of course, I thought sometimes when I was down there that he looked pretty drawn and a little bit peaky. And he was always having problems with is stomach, you know. And this may have been—Tom was, you know, a great finagler. I remember the business of snoring to get to sleep outside the dormitory. Well, you know, they had, the poor guys, they all had to sleep in this great big cattle barn where they didn't have separate rooms, they were just sort of six-foot high partitions and then these nasty little bunks. And Tom didn't like it a bit. And he thought of a scheme—a clever fellow, he thought of the idea of learning to snore very loudly. And he did. He learned how to snore very loudly and the monks in chapter said that Father Louis had to get out of there, that they couldn't stand his snoring. So he got moved to one of the old bishop's rooms up in the front of the building there.

MERTON'S
ORDINATION

I think you said you liked the poems of Mr. Howard, so I'll copy out for you one he sent me that I like a lot. It's about Vienna in the good old days before they got Socialism. I wish I could write a poem like that but I'm too lazy to read up for it. One thing puzzles me a bit; the capybara, the world's largest edible rodent. Is Mr. Howard a symbolist, or is he just like Marianne Moore, queer for arcane animals?

I used to take Miss Moore to the ball games. She knew everything there was to know about baseball, even more than that. She had seen Bobby Thompson hit his famous tie-breaking homer at the Polo Grounds. But I could tie her on that; I had seen Mazerozki's famous homer over the scoreboard at Forbes Field when the Pirates beat the Yankees. That was the same game when the Yankee's great shortstop Phil Rizzuto was hit in the Adam's apple and he had to be taken out. Phil Rizzuto is now on TV pitching 10% loans for the Money Store. How the mighty . . .

Miss Moore was a Livin' Doll, and the Soul of Kindness, but she did go on and on when she telephoned. Mostly she talked about Ezra's predicament and what could be done about it.

Miss Moore—I always called her Miss—applied the precision she learned as editor of *The Dial* to the syllabic patterns of her poems, to her social life and to baseball. She could have managed the Dodgers.

NABOKOV

NABOKOV'S
NOTE TO
HIS NIKOLAI
GOGOL
ND, 1959

"Well," said my publisher . . .

A delicate sunset was framed in a golden gap between gaunt mountains. The remote rims of the gap were eye lashed with firs and still further, deep in the gap itself, one could distinguish the silhouettes of other, lesser and quite ethereal, mountains. We were in Utah, sitting in the lounge of an Alpine hotel. The slender aspens on the near slopes and the pale pyramids of ancient mine dumps took advantage of the plateglass window to participate silently in our talk—somewhat in the same way as the Byronic pictures did in regard to the dialogue in Sobakevich's house.

"Well,"—said my publisher,—"I like it—but I do think the student ought to be told what it is all about."

I said . . . —"No," he said, "I don't mean that. I mean the student ought to be told more about Gogol's books. I mean the plots. He would want to know what those books are about."

I said . . . —"No, you have not," he said.—"I have gone through it carefully and so has my wife, and we have not found the plots. There should also be some kind of bibliography or chronology at the end. The student ought to be able to find his way, otherwise he would be puzzled and would not bother to read any further."

I said that an intelligent person could always look up dates and things in a good encyclopedia or in any manual of Russian literature. He said that a student would not be necessarily an intelligent person and anyway would resent the trouble of having to look up things. I said there were students and students. He said that from a publisher's point of view there was only one sort.

"I have tried to explain,"—I said,—"that in Gogol's books the real plots are behind the obvious ones. Those real plots I do give.

His stories only mimic stories with plots. It is like a rare
moth that departs from a moth-like appearance to mimic the
superficial pattern of a structurally quite different thing—
some popular butterfly, say. "That's all right,"—he said.

"Or rather unpopular, unpopular with lizards and birds."

"Yes, I understand,"—he said.—"I understand perfectly well.
But after all a plot is a plot, and the student must be told what
happens. *For instance, until I read* The Government Inspector
myself I had not the slightest idea what it was all about although
I had studied your manuscript." "Tell me,"—I asked,—"what hap-
pens in The Inspector General?"

"Well," —he said, throwing himself back in his chair,—"what
happens is that a young man gets stranded in a town because
he had lost all his money at cards, and the town is full of
politicians, and he uses the politicians to raise some money by
making them believe that he is a Government official sent from
headquarters to inspect them. And when he has used them, and
made love to the Mayor's daughter, and drunk the Mayor's wine,
and accepted bribes from judges and doctors and landowners
and merchants and all kinds of administrators, he leaves the
town, just before the real inspector arrives." I said . . .

"Yes, of course you may use it,"—said my publisher
cooperatively.—"Then there is also Dead Souls. *I could not tell*
what it is all about after reading your chapter. And then, as I say,
there ought to be a bibliography."

"If you mean a list of translations and books on Gogol . . ."
"Well,"—said my publisher.

"If you want that, the matter is simple, for except Guerney's
excellently rendered Dead Souls, The Inspector General *and*
The Overcoat, *which appeared while I was myself wrestling with*

them, there exists nothing but ridiculously garbled versions."

At this point two cocker puppies, a draggle-eared black one with an appealing slant in the bluish whites of his eyes and a little white bitch with a pink-dappled face and belly, tumbled in through the door someone had opened, stumbled about on padded paws in between the furniture and were promptly caught and banished again to their place on the terrace.

"Otherwise,"—I went on,—"I know of no English work on Gogol worth listing except Mirsky's excellent chapter in his History of Russian Literature (Knopf, New York). Of course, there are hundreds of Russian works. Of these a few are very good, but lots of others belong to the preposterous schools of "Gogol the Painter of Tsarist Russia" or "Gogol the Realist" or "Gogol the Great Opposer of Serfdom and Bureaucracy" or "Gogol the Russian Dickens." The trouble is that if I start listing these works, I am sure to try to allay my boredom by inserting here and there fictitious titles and imaginary authors so that you will never quite know whether Dobrolubov or Ivanov-Razumnik or Ovsyano Kuli—" "No,"—said my publisher hastily.—"I don't think that a list of books on Gogol is necessary. What I meant, was a list of Gogol's own books with a sequence of dates and a chronology of his doings, and something about the plots and so on. You could easily do this. And we must have Gogol's picture."

"I have been thinking of that myself,"—I said. "Yes—let us have a picture of Gogol's nose. Not his face and shoulders, etc. but only his nose. A big solitary sharp nose—neatly outlined in ink like the enlarged figure of some important part of a curious zoological specimen. I might ask Dobuzhinsky, that unique master of the line, or perhaps a Museum artist . . ."

"And it would kill the book,"—said my publisher.

Volodya is correct. Volya is my abbreviation of that. Of course, I never addressed his nobility as that, but that's the way I thought of him.

Volya was a doll in a very severe, upper-crust Russian way.

I wanted to be his friend, but he didn't want any jejune ninkapoop to be his friend. He wanted big brains such as Wilson and Levin to be his friends. It was Levin who put me in touch with him. He had Vera write his terse little letters to me. He would force a smile for me sometimes but it was a long-ways-away smile. The real smile was still on the flatcar that was transporting his grandfather's carriage and horses across Europe for the summer vacation at Biarritz. He declared that in his *Gogol* there were three pulls of my leg, but I've never been able to find them—and he wouldn't tell.

What you don't understand is that at the time he wrote *Lolita*, this was a dirty book. I was very fond of him. He'd spent the summer with me in the Alta Lodge, out hunting butterflies. His nice wife was there and the child, the innocent child. I wrote saying: "Volya, you are so sophisticated, you may not realize the effect that this book is going to have on the college community of Cornell if you publish it. Your wife will be ostracized, stones will be thrown at your child." He said, "Well, maybe, what'll I do with it?" I suggested that he send it to Girodias at the Obelisk Press in Paris. College communities are so awful, some of them, in that respect—no tolerance. Maybe they're better now; I don't know. I remember that I used to visit with L.R. Lind at the University of Kansas. Before we could have a drink, he had to pull down the shades in the room. This was my slant on the college communities.

LAUGHTER in the DARK

VLADIMIR NABOKOV

NARRAGANSETT

Nummusquaunamuckqunmanit.
That's "God is angry with me" in Narragansett.

(Vide Roger Williams: *A Key into the Language of America.*)

Next question:
Tunna-awwa commitchichunck-kitonckquean?
"Wither goes your soul when you die?"

NEW DIRECTIONS

Although Pound wrote and talked about Henry James it was "Matty" who started me reading James systematically. It's hard to believe today but in the Thirties and Forties James was little read. There were other similar cases of great writers who had dropped out of fashion after their deaths. Scribner had not kept Scott Fitzgerald in print. For a few years I was able to lease the rights to *The Great Gatsby* from them for my "New Classics" series. When Fitzgerald's literary executor Edmund Wilson put together the *Crack-Up* collection it was turned down by all the big New York publishers. It fell to me in 1945 and quickly went through several printings. There was a similar situation with E.M. Forster. When I began doing revivals only *A Passage to India,* a Harcourt Brace book, was in print. Alfred Knopf had been his original and regular publisher. There was gossip that Alfred had lost interest because Forster had forgotten a lunch date in London. Goodness knows good old Alfred, my idol in publishing who later became a close friend, was touchy, offending many people, but I think this anecdote is apocryphal. Be that as it may, I was able to lease *The Longest Journey* and *A Room with a View* for a number of years. These leases, of course, were cancelled, when the original publishers took note of the sales figures on the New Directions royalty reports. Other revivals that came my way were Evelyn Waugh's *A Handful of Dust* and Céline's two great classics *Death on the Installment Plan* and *Journey to the End of the Night,* the two Célines happily still on our list in modernized translations.

NIN, ANAÏS

Anaïs Nin don't like James Laughlin

I'm sorry that I never actually met Lorine Niedecker. From her many letters over the years I think of her as an old friend. She was an original in the best sense, hoeing her own row in poetry with complete disregard for literary fashion. She seldom left her hometown of Fort Atkinson, Wisconsin, where, I'm told, few people knew that she was a poet.

At the time of her death in 1970 I wrote of her: "She was the genuine U.S. article, a person who knew what she wanted to do and did it." [Here is] the echt Niedecker flavor:

My life is hung up
in the flood
a wave-blurred
portrait

Don't fall in love
with this face—
it no longer exists
in water
we cannot fish.

NORFOLK

Dear Stan,

*I'm trying to think of people here who might dislike
Bush enough to contribute.*

*Our neighbor Alex Vagliano runs 300 sheep which he markets
to Arabs in NYC. But everyone knows that he makes his money
with a Telex hooked to Zurich on which he does arbitrage with a
Herr Gut. Alex was doing well at Morgan—he set up their branch
in Milan. But when he was passed over for a top job he quit. His
third wife, Sara, is an ex-Princeton professor of French. She has
the most beautiful garden in Norfolk. I give her $1000 a year for
Planned Parenthood (in memory of Ann) so she kind of owes me,
though I wouldn't quite put it that way. The Vagliano phone
is 542-5539.*

*The best-read man in Norfolk, and the one with the best
manners, is Robertson F. Alford, Doolittle Lake, Norfolk.
(542-5114) I only see them about twice a year because they spend
most of their time at a place in Tuscany. I can't imagine that a
man who knows everything about every culture would like Bush.
However, his wife raises Bessarabian hounds in Italy. That may
be a bad sign.*

*Cousin Ted (Edward C.) Childs, Barbara Lawrence's father—
our common ancestor was Colonel James Childs of the 10th
Pennsylvania Cavalry, who had his head hit by a cannonball at
Antietam but fortunately he had thought to impregnate his wife
before going off to the battle—Cousin Ted, generally recognized
as the Duke of Norfolk, is "comfortably off." He holds 7000 acres
of woodland which he would like to give to the state for a forest
but they are too broke to accept it without an endowment.
His father Starling, an investment banker put together Texas
Utilities, Montana Power, Long Island Lighting and Florida
Power & Light, and his wife was the daughter of Mr. Coffin who*

helped start General Electric . . . yes, Cousin Ted is "comfortably
off"—and his generosity to the town is only equaled by his desire
for anonymity—but when I attended his 89th birthday party the
other day and tried to draw him into conversation about Bush,
he didn't seem quite certain of who George Bush was, though he
remembered a "very nice chap" named "Press Bush" at Yale. . . .
So perhaps the Duke is not a good prospect.

In South Norfolk there is a banker (of French extraction) who
has loaned too much money to Brazil, by name Allain Saman, Old
Goshen Road. I smile at his 6-foot wife in the post office, but he
wouldn't know me from Adam.

West of us, in Canaan, there is the widow of Robert Montgomery,
the actor. I forget her first name, a most intelligent lady who is
now somewhat reclusive.

In Taconic is someone I'm sure you know from Washington,
the widow (Anne) of "Pete" Scoville (Herbert), who was in arms
control. Anne is very highminded and an accomplished sculptor
in metals. When she and Pete became engaged Aunt Leila gave
a dance for them in the big room at Robin Hill.

Meryl Streep has sold her place in Salisbury and returned to
LA. A wonderful actress, but she has a hard time getting parts
now because of her age.

I'm sure you know the various Buckleys in Sharon. I'm told by
a reliable source that the publisher of the conservative magazine,
who wrote that scandalous book about Yale in his youth, puts
drops in his eyes to make them flash before he appears for his
show on TV.

The great leverager Henry Kravitz has bought a big spread
over near Litchfield, but from his activities I assume
he's a friend of Bush.

Two people whom Ann greatly admired, and I too, are the Robert H. Meads (Henrietta) at Yale Farm, Norfolk. He raises cattle (Angus, I think) and his hobby is coaching wrestling at Salisbury School. They are "old" Norfolk, a 100% all right couple. Should be on to Bush.

I think that about exhausts my knowledge of the Norfolk area financial topography. I've rambled on. Dr. Wiesel has put me on Prozac for my depression; it cheers me up but makes me babbulous.

NORFOLK

We all do our duty.
I have agreed to do
a Thursday evening
at the Country Club
if I may read ancient
Greek poems in
translation. That
should stiffen a few
chins for the struggle
against Gingrich.

NEW YORK TIMES

To the Editor,

*Re some perhaps over-generous remarks on page 30, your
issue of November 2nd, may I without Disrespect advert that:*

MY FAVORITE NEWSPAPER

*is always up to date could it be
that they have a computer program-*

*med to choose their book reviewers
like the ones they use at dating*

*services (are you a remarkable sin-
gle looking for an equally remark*

*able single?) unfortunately in my
case there was a snafu the computer*

*must have had my name spelled wrong
and I drew the expert on cholesterol-*

*free salad dressings well better
luck next time perhaps Rupert Mur-*

*doch has a smarter machine that
will deal me a rave in the* Post.

But I do think that if the young feller (whose poetry I admire)
wants to make it in literary criticism he should do his homework.
The line in Spanish which he brings up is not by Machado de
Assis, the Brazilian novelist, but by the Spanish poet Antonio
Machado. They talk Portuguese down there in Rio.

James Laughlin
Norfolk, Conn.

OLSON, CHARLES

I must get the Olson CP. He never got over arriving at 2AM in Eliot House hoping to sleep in Ted Spencer's (empty of Ted) bed and finding me already in it. Of such monumental events . . .

OPPEN

WOW! Guess who won the Pulitzer Prize for Poetry! Our little old George Oppen. Totally a surprise, but nice . . . His sales on the book which won were *negative* for 1968, i.e.—more returns than sales. Salesmen begged me last year—"No more Oppen, *please*"—we just can't sell him. Waiting to see their Rosey Visages this Thursday at Sales Meeting in Phila. One never knows who Pulitzer judges are. (But Jim Dickey leaked he was this year, but said he was going to vote for Patchen.)

OPPENS

I've just had a tender letter from George Oppen's sister, she of the rapturous Semitic pulchritude and pashun. She dates back to 1941, and has since been married four times. She laments the passing of our youths. We went out to camp in the flowers in the desert below Tonapah, Nevada. She couldn't even fry an egg (very rich the Oppenheimers, they went to Monte Carlo every winter). George was such a sweet man. And then the bad ending of Alzheimers. Rexroth was jealous of him and spread the canard that it was he who murdered Trotsky, just because George and Mary were having a vacation in Mexico. (Rexroth had a wicked tongue.)

I'm so pleased that you liked the poem about June Oppen. Rexroth gave her a hard time. He was always pursuing her, making a fool of himself. I remember one night looking in the window of June's apartment. There was Kenneth, fully clad, trying to make her drink champagne out of one of her slippers.

No, I didn't know that you and George Oppen were particularly close. A lovely man with a unique kind of charm. It was a sweetness. His gentle nature shows in the poems, at least for me.

It would indeed be interesting to get at George's papers. The stuff that is in San Diego. It will be unfortunate if that material falls into the hands of a PhD maggot. Can't you train up a disciple who could undertake the task under your supervision, so that there could be a little humanity in the text presented?

One thing I remember vividly about George. He happened to be in New York when Ezra was on one of his visits. I got the two of them together in my office. George was so moved to be again at the foot of his master all he could do was cry. It was very moving.

OMAHA

The Boy publisher loaded up his ancient Buick with books and headed west. Go west, young man; I did. In three weeks I covered the big cities as far out as Minneapolis and Omaha.

These trips were exhausting, and often disheartening, but I learned a great deal about American Civilization. And I found that there were a few kind hearts in every town. Imagine, if you will, that you are the lady bookbuyer in Halle's Department Store in Cleveland, one of the best in the land. Suddenly you are confronted by a bizarre apparition: a frighteningly tall young man in an Austrian Lodenmantel, his eyes aflame, who tells you that almost all of the books in your department are junk and that your customers should be reading some nut over in Italy and an obscure pediatrician in Rutherford, New Jersey. An experience to spoil a whole day. But none of these ladies ever called security to fetch a straitjacket. And they had good hearts. I would leave these magnificent emporia with an order for one or two copies of each book I had offered—not enough to pay for gas for the guzzling Buick, let alone my B & B at a tourist home (there were no motels in those days), but enough to give hope to battle on another day. *In hac spe vivit.*

Cleveland was a dream city compared with Omaha. Why did I go to Omaha? I guess because it was on the map. There was Mathews Book Store and in it, breathing flame, was Mrs. Martha Mathews. Medea? More so. Medusa? More than she. From Mrs. Mathews I came away unrequited with smile or pence. She did not throw me out—she was petite. She simply retired to the lavatory and stayed there till I left. Yet I returned to Omaha. Mrs. Mathews was my challenge. I felt that if I could crack Mrs. Mathews a new day would dawn for American writers. But in three visits I never sold her a book. *Die heilige Martha der Schlachthöfe.*

OLGA RUDGE

When I first came to Rapallo in the fall of 1934 to study in Pound's "Ezuversity," I didn't know my way around or who was who. So when I spotted a very goodlooking young lady sitting by herself at a café table I didn't hesitate to ask if I might join her. She was vivacious and told good anecdotes about Max Beerbohm and other famous personalities who had lived in Rapallo. I was puzzled by her accent and asked if she were English. No, she said, she had been born in Youngstown, Ohio, but the family had moved to England when she was quite young. I sat with her other days but noticed that she was never at her table on Tuesdays or Fridays. I learned more a few weeks later when I had become friendly with Gerhardt Muench, the young German pianist whom Pound had urged to settle in Rapallo to play in the concerts Ezra sponsored in the municipio. "Weisst du nicht, dass diese Dame Ezras Besitzt ist?"... Don't you know that the lady belongs to Ezra? A fact which was confirmed a few days later when I happened to be in the "main drain" of the

town, the first big street back of the seafront plazas. There came Ezra, dressed to the nines in his velvet jacket, pants with equestrian seat, his cowboy hat, swinging his silver-headed cane as he made for San Ambrogio, women applauding him from their windows. It was one of the sights of the town. Olga, that was her name, lived up the mountainside, renting the first floor of a peasant house near the little church of San Pantaleone. The view up there over the Ligurian Gulf was marvelous and the whole area was covered with olive trees. There were no car roads up there then; the climb up the stony salita was arduous. Ezra's concerts in the town hall were very fine. Olga, with her violin, was the lead player, with Muench and occasional imported talent filling in. The program was usually Mozart and Vivaldi, Olga's favorite composer. Vivaldi was the master of Italian Baroque music. In later years she became a scholar of Vivaldi, researching his unpublished scores in Turin and Dresden. She turned up over 300 unplayed Vivaldi concerti, arranging to get some of them published.

PUBLISHING

Biznizz stinks worse than ever. I am learning to care deeply for the gin. This is probably a bad thing, but what to do . . .

These days ND is abubble with a frenetic roil of switched wires and tangled gargles as we struggle to get out a lot of new books. Ruin hangs like a large garbage pail over the Halloween doorway because costs are way up and sales are way down. But who knows, who ever knows, who does?

important and gratifying: keeping all the books of Pound and William Carlos Williams in print, which I could do because I inherited money. A normal commercial publisher would have had to remainder many books ND keeps in print.

Of course, as you know, the condition of the book trade is lamentable. The chains work on a quick-in, quick-out basis. I've heard that some of them are trying to be better about inventory but I haven't seen it with my own eyes. The days of the old Mom & Pop bookstore, people usually who were really interested in literature, are departing. Those couples don't have the financing to float an extensive inventory. Since we are all, I'm told, going to be on the information super-highway, reading off our little screens with musical accompaniment of rock 'n roll, it hardly matters.

PUBLISHING, C. 1936

You wouldn't believe how dreary it was for the avant-garde writers at that time. What changed it really in the end was simply the dying off of the old English professors. They gradually died, or retired—let's say they retired.

POETRY

It is estimated that there are over 100,000 poets in the USA, and I would like to be one of them.

Perhaps I shd be more cheerful. My 1986 check from City Lights for the S.P. was $1690. More than a lot of ND poets get. Bilis ed dubitatio est. Do they buy the book for the nice cover? For the funny paper poems? My metric is so eccentric how many can even hear the cadence in the lines? I have become my metric. Like doubling. Virgil said: Trahit sua quemque voluptas." And Propertius: "Ingenium nobis ipsa puella facit." All that sentimentality. I'm too old to change. Yes, I have been lucky, with some exceptions.

PARRA

Parra, who now that Neruda is dead, is Chile's leading living poet . . . Parra was a leftist who found the bourgeoisie as ridiculous as had the Dadaists. He rebelled against the overstuffed traditions of earlier Latin-American poetry. His tone is humorously bitter. And he favors the poetic statement which verges on nonsense.

PITTSBURGH

There was not much "gracious living" in Pittsburgh, where at one house, the butler passed chewing gum on a silver salver after the coffee.

The only bunch I liked were the Howes in a grand house called Benedum. He was the first to make money out of Pennsylvania oil. There were fourteen children, but one of the girls died of appendicitis because she wouldn't take her medicine. The old man was a religious scholar. If things got noisy when he was trying to work he would emerge from his study and holler "Zion triumphant!" Then there was silence for a while.

Woodland Road centered around Pennsylvania College for Women. An early institution to take females seriously. Later it became Chatham College. No architectural distinction except a pretty copy of a white New England church. It says over the door "James Laughlin Memorial Library," named for my great-grandfather. They don't buy ND books so I shun them. The college has a big steep hill in front of it. We were allowed to sled and ski on it. That's where I did my first skiing on long boards with only toe-straps to hold the foot down.

My brother didn't want it, he was based in Phila, so I gave my mother's house to Chatham. There are 40 girls living in it. At evening the sweet odor of pot drifts out of it. We sold Big Springs the lovely place in the Alleghenies to a man who has made a fish hatchery out of it.

My natal city, rebuilt by the Mellons, has become a veritable Dioce. Yet it depresses me. The JL Library at Chatham College has 1 Pound book. (The building, the donation of *mon arrière grandpère*. And where his house stood, with the gardens running to the river, is a Ph. Johnson gothic skyscraper built of glass. Cute little spires of glass.) Oh well.

PLIMPTON

Which brings me to the subject of George and the problem of the right interviewer. Because of his social jitterbugging and his doing TV commercials in his Boston accent George has his detractors. Some call him the male Jackie-O. But I think he's a serious character. When that bunch of boys finished Cambridge and went to Paris to start *Paris Review*, he was the one who really put the magazine together and kept it going. I think he invented the interview format. He takes them very seriously and works very hard on them. I saw that when he did the 2-part interview on me. It was done by a jerk and George did a lot of good shaping and rewrite. He maintains standards.

PARTIES

I don't do very well at cocktail parties. But I went to this one, in New York in 1942, because it was given by Lincoln Kirstein, who has been one of my great culture heroes since 1933, when he began publishing *Hound & Horn* (not a hunting but a brilliant literary magazine, which Pound, who tried to infiltrate it, called the *Bitch & Bugle*).

Lincoln gives fine parties but my luck held poor. In his lovable way, Lincoln assured me that the best book New Directions had ever published was Baron Corvo's *Desire and Pursuit of the Whole*. Lionel Trilling, whom I had persuaded to write his brilliant book about E.M. Forster, thought I was George L.K. Morris, the abstract painter. Lincoln introduced me to Roger Stevens—the fourth time I'd met him—and the great father figure of the theater blessed me with the same stare of complete nonrecognition.

Then in the gallery room, by himself and as if trying to fade into the wall, I saw a not-large, youngish blonde man in a rumpled gray sweater who seemed to be having as hard a time as I was. It was Tennessee Williams. We got to talking and discovered that we were both great fans of the poets Hart Crane and Rilke. Tennessee told me that he never travelled anywhere without the poems of Crane in his knapsack. Those were the days before fame and airplanes for him, when he did most of his trips by hitchhiking.

POETS

Where do mediocre poets get my home address? Their junk keeps turning up and some don't send envs. Too many bad poets.

Many writers, especially poets, whom ND did not publish disliked me very much.

POVERTY

I can't remember whether or not we discussed the grisly matter of the contract with the Pound Trust. Their lawyer has pretty stiff rules on what can be done. On the clothbound, out of a total royalty of 15%, the Trust takes 10%, and allocates to the editor a royalty of 5%, but with a cut-off point, to make certain that he is kept in perpetual poverty, as befits a literary man.

PRINCETON

It nearly broke my father's heart when I didn't go to Princeton. Like so many in Pittsburgh ours was a Princeton family. My grandfather had been a trustee of Princeton and gave the university a dormitory, Laughlin Hall—it's still there—one of those pseudo-Gothic creations built of fieldstone which symbolized learning. He also gave the farmlands east of the campus to which the university has now expanded, happily not in the old architectural style.

As soon as my brother and I were able to behave ourselves we were taken along with many cousins to Princeton class reunions in June. We loved the parades with the college band going on before. We were given little straw boaters with my father's class numerals, 1900, or "oughty-ought" as that year was called, on the bands and orange-and-black pennants to wave. Usually we were housed at the Nassau Inn where there was the attraction of an outdoor swimming pool. Some years there was a tiger in the parade, not a real tiger, of course, but a student cavorting in a tiger skin.

My brother was five years older than I and most of the time quite horrid to the spoiled brat. But he did not disappoint. He sailed through Princeton, making Tiger Inn, one of the most important clubs, and he was Second All-American fullback on the soccer team. There was only one blot on his record; he wrote his senior paper on Proust, a degenerate, a no-no author in Pittsburgh. Could this lapse have derived from the fact that in 1929 we were sent to a boarding school in Switzerland to prevent our being upset by events connected with the Great Depression? In later years my maternal grandfather often remarked that it was most unfortunate that we had been exposed to "medical knowledge" in Europe. But my brother's brush with decadence did not destroy his career. He went into the family steel business, into sales, and was well liked by the customers. And he was well liked by the Navy for which he was purchasing officer in the metals division during the war. And he was faithful to Princeton. After he was moved to the Philadelphia office he seldom missed a football game in Palmer Stadium. His house was a menagerie of tigers of all kinds and sizes. On one visit I counted twenty-six tigers, beginning with a tiger doormat and a tiger knocker. Paintings of tigers, a tapestry tiger, china tigers, bronze tigers, fierce tigers, comical tigers . . .

But it was Harvard for me, not Princeton.

PYJAMAS

Speaking of "jammies," did I recount the great little epigram tossed to me by the granddaughter of P. Claudel, dramatist, the lady I liked best at Drue's fiesta? I was telling her how when in Paris I always wore my red ribbon which deterred the ladies at the Postes from cheating me so badly on stamps for my letters. She asked: "why don't you have the ribbon sewn to your pyjamas?" Quick, them kaffolix.

PULITZER

Freshman year drastically altered my lifestyle. At home in Pittsburgh there had been no smoking; Father and my uncles did their drinking, if any, at the Duquesne Club and because I felt too shy and awkward to go to children's dances the only girls I knew were my cousins. Each morning there were family prayers (with the servants standing at attention, except the Catholic ones who were excused); Sundays there was Sunday school, then Church, my maternal grandfather gave me a dime if I had mastered my page of the Westminster Catechism, and evenings there was the Bible game (questions from scripture on cards) and hymn singing with the player piano.

A fellow whom I'll call Talbot changed all that. He taught me to smoke, to drink and to have impure thoughts about girls. Talbot had a great destiny before him, in the field of communication but he seemed to be doing nothing to ready himself for it. All his courses were at the Fogg Art Museum or in the music department. When the next year, he moved on from the Yard to Eliot House, he had the largest suite in the complex with a grand piano on which he played Chopin and Liszt with some talent. On the walls were French paintings: Dufy (the Montmartre fellow), Marie Laurencin, and a stunning Odilon Redon flower painting. (Later in life, Talbot told me that he had "the finest Picassos west of the Mississippi.") Talbot was tall, handsome in a somnolent way and moved with languor. He spoke in a rather affected languid drawl. He teased me constantly and could be most sardonic. I can still see the way he twisted his lips when he was going to be sardonic. Sophistication was his code. All of this had not come from the city where he had grown up. With his family, he had spent much time in France. He knew French well. His favorite authors were Huysmans, Montesquieu and Proust. His suits were made in London and he would never wear ready-made shoes. His footgear came from Jermyn St. He was definitely not gay.

PULITZER

Joe Pulitzer at Harvard (as per Slocum)

JP: J, you look as if you were made of green jade.
JL: Well, that's good enough.
JP: Good enough for some people.

Sign on JP's door in Eliot House during the reading period:
If you want to communicate, call the Ritz in N.Y.

PRESENCE OF AN ABSENCE

I'm a turnip head. When you speak of an "imaginary space, the presence of an absence . . ." I'm pushed back to the confusion I had when trying to read the books Merton had quoted in the *Asian Journal*, to get it fixed up for the printer, it came to me in the notes state, a little tag on his small satchel which read: "In the event of my death this case to be delivered to James Laughlin," and two years I swam in a sea of ignorance trying to figure all those strange ideas out . . . and specifically "the presence of an absence" takes me back to that night in Trivandarum (did you ever see the poem?) when the fiery old guru, he looked like Oswald Spengler made of black bronze, asked me, "Now you, Mr. America, with your Aristotle, what is in the space between two thoughts?" *Vedanta*—I hadn't the foggiest, and he would not tell me the answer.

POUND

When I was twenty I had the good luck to attend for two terms
of several months each what Pound liked to call the "Ezuversity"
in Rapallo. He and his wife were living then in the fifth floor
rooftop flat which looked out over the Tigullian Bay. The building was on the seafront but one entered at number 12 in the narrow old Via Marsala. Back of the big terrace there were four or
five small rooms furnished with the simplicity Pound always preferred: many of the chairs and tables he had constructed himself
from odd bits of wood picked up at the local carpentry-shops.
The handsome Gaudier sculptures were there, small but
extremely fine pieces, and among the paintings a remarkable
Max Ernst, a beautiful abstraction of two white conch shells. In
Dorothy Pound's sitting room there were Wyndham Lewis colored drawings and several of her own very talented sketches.
Books along the lower part of the walls on homemade shelves.

LUNCH IN
RAPALLO

But not as many as one would have expected. Pound was always very selective and got rid of those that would not qualify for "the canon" (my term). Of his own workplace, the little study between the entryway and Mrs. Pound's sitting room, I remember the ordering of what would otherwise have been a clutter. Current filing of worldwide correspondence was done on spindles or in clip folders ranged along the wall behind his desk chair. Pencils and scissors hung on strings from the ceiling so they could not get lost in the papers on his desk. (Pound's postage bill must certainly have been his largest expense at that time.)

I was troubled because at all the conferences there were almost no undergraduates. Just Poundians and curious oldsters. Are the galloping termites driving them away? Or do the *Cantos* just not speak to them? I recall that Eliot took a big nosedive at one point with the young. Will Helen Vendler convince them that Jimmy Merrill is better than Duncan?

Does Widener have a copy of that Italian picture book of the del Cosa frescoes in the Schifanoia palace at Ferrara?

As you know, Ezra was much influenced for the structure of the Cantos *by the "zones" in the frescoes: the virtues, the seasons, and the scenes of contemporary life.*

POUND

It really doesn't matter, does it, whether EP knew what he was doing? But that gets us into areas I don't like. Well, he did it.

Emily Wallace, who was on Terry's Sacred Places tour, says Boris took over the group when they came to the castle and gave them the princely routine. He took them to see a stuffed horse at some barracks. Is that in the *Cantos*? I can't find this horse in the concordance.

I remember the fuss we were in when Ezra was brought to Washington and we didn't know what to do about it. Both Eliot and Dorothy were in favor of the insanity approach so we went for that. But it was a long stay that he had at the government's expense. I would get down to see him now and then and he always seemed remarkably cheerful. After all, they took good care of him, feeding him well and letting Dorothy come in for lunches. He was allowed guests as long as they weren't journalists. He didn't have to worry about much except for the destruction of the world.

. . . DON'T take your chewing gum and candy money to pay me. What, NO! The aged shd. not sponge on the next generation. . . . I think you better stick with Hawvud a bit longer. I mean, don't leave the country prematurely/you might have to return later in life. You were??? 18?? last summer . . .

EP TO JL

ALBERGO RAPALLO

PASSEGGIATA MARE

RAPALLO - Telef. 8357

Via Marsde

12 /5 —

Am here till

No 28ᵗʰ or

29ᵗʰ

visibility high.

you can also

have opportunity

of playing

SLAYING

POUND FILM

The brash young (Oxonian) producer from London Weekend Television who projects a film on EP starring Burt Lancaster was here for a day. The script is about what you'd expect—sensational and tawdry. Mary is the heroine, Dorothy is tight-lipped, Olga is caricatured, and Ezra is a fool. Marcella is libeled. After 6 hours I may or may not have convinced him he would ruin his career putting out such trash. At least he promised to get Burt out of bed (sic) with Olga. The Trust lawyer says little can be done to stop it as Ez is a "public figure" and dead at that—Quotes from *Cantos* are the only good part. But I think Marcella could sue.

I wish there were a photo of Hon George Tinkham riding his horse into the bar to put on the screen, but there isn't. Luminous details.

The showing of the film in Chicago went well. No placards. The only person who walked out was an elderly gent who from his haste appeared to have either a prostatic or diarrhetic problem.

However, the question period bogged down with one of those serious types who asked whether poets should get into politics, quoting Shelley. I advised him not to run either against the Senegambian incumbent or the Irish lady. Not enough registered poets.

EP AS
A DANCING
MAIDEN IN A
GREEK PLAY
AT PENN

POUND

THE SIXTH MERMAID

Not something we should chat with the innocent students about, but this question came to me as I looked it up for a note for my "roaring sea" tag poem, where I won't put it either.

Who was the sixth mermaid?

This reads pretty clear to me, that after behaving himself for some years after his marriage to Dorothy, Ezra got tired of that frigidity (DP once expressed to me sentiments similar to those of my revered mother, who didn't care for the "unpleasant" side of marriage) and took off after the sirens.

1. Would be Bridget Patmore, to whom Dorothy always referred as that "dreadful woman."

2. Would be Bride Scratton who killed herself for abandoned love of Ez.

3. Would be Iris Barry, to whom he wrote some fine instructional letters, but she fled to NYC and became a functionary of film at the MoMA.

4. Could be Agnes Bedford, W. Lewis' pal, who later helped Ez score his operas.

5. Would doubtlessly be Nancy Cunard (or her ma, or both together) who was all over the lot, and must have been a real nut but is kindly mentioned in the *Cantos*, and our boy WCW may, or may not, have gotten his finger caught in that cookie jar.

6. ??? But it may come to me . . .

PATCHEN, KENNETH

Sometimes it is strange what the memory retains. Where are the pieces that the film editor cut and dropped on the cutting room floor? I think I knew Kenneth Patchen for about thirty-three-years. That would be from old letters; I never kept a diary. And the scenes of Miriam and Kenneth which survive are not in narrative sequence. They jump around in time, a flickering black and white film. There isn't much sound, though I can hear Kenneth's deep, deliberately slow voice and Miriam's liquid laughter. Surely it must have been Miriam's laughter which kept Kenneth going through those years of agony when his back was constant pain and the pain was battering his spirit.

The first scene shows Patchen and his young wife Miriam at the Oikemuses' farm near Concord, Massachusetts. That would be in 1938. I had been corresponding with Kenneth for over a year; I was impressed by his first book of poems, *Before the Brave*, which Random House published in 1936. The writer of the jacket copy, who was not off the mark, spoke of Patchen's "social and revolutionary principles," and said that "he scorns the devices of his poetic elders and seeks by experimentation new and more dynamic verse forms." Not exactly Bennett Cerf's kind of book, but it certainly was mine. So I was happy when Random House let him go and he signed on with New Directions. His first book with us was *First Will and Testament* in 1939.

But back to the farm. I noted how very tidy the Oikemuses kept their place. If the edges of the picture are out of focus, the center is not. Miriam was, and is, more than pretty. There is the light from within, the radiance of the illuminated heart. And Kenneth, before illness demolished him, was a handsome man. Those eyes were gentle, but there was such an intensity in his glance. He always looked at people, not around them. He looked into me and sometimes I hated to think of what he might be seeing there. Miriam had told me that her parents, who came from Finland, were socialists. One reason I came to Concord was to look into that; I was planning to ask the Patchens to come run the New

Directions office in Norfolk. It was on the family place, which was presided over by that miraculous survivor from an earlier age, my Aunt Leila. She was a lady of infinite good works, but her social and political views were somewhat retarded. Once I had met the Patchens, and the Oikemuses, I knew there would be no problem. They were not *Reds*. They were fine people, good people; they were pacifists.

QUENEAU

1. I'm pretty sure that the Queneau is around here somewhere but I think Julia the cleaning lady has hidden it as she does . . .

2. Fascinating, but it would bankrupt us—and nobody would buy it.

QUINNEY

I have been privileged to know a few great and good men in my life, and Joe Quinney was unique among them. For clarity of mind, for dedication in every task, and for a very practical benevolence, we shall not see his equal. Once when we were fishing in the Snake River Joe told me stories of his young days as a Mormon missionary in Germany. I've always thought that that experience gave his character its set. But he wasn't rigid or sectarian.

Joe was, I think, the last survivor of the small group of Salt Lake men who love to ski and, encouraged by Mayor George Watson, had a vision of what a skiers' paradise Alta could become. They persuaded the Forest Service to build the highway, they raised money from the Denver & Rio Grande Railroad to build the old Alta Lodge, and they built the first Collins Lift with phone poles for towers and parts salvaged from the Michigan Utah mine. We all owe so much to those men—Bill O'Connor, Stu Cosgriff, Paul Keyser, Perc Kittel and the rest. But we owe most to Joe Quinney. Alta became his favorite hobby and his constant concern. He skied its slopes and he was its business brain. For years, each Tuesday, he would meet in his office with Fred Speyer and Chic Morton to solve problems and go over plans. If Alta is a great ski resort today—and if it still has a $10 day pass —it is thanks to those three great men, and chief among them Joe.

Joe was always modest. His satisfactions were interior. Once when we had built a new lift I suggested that it be named for him. He would have none of that. But Alta will always be his living memorial. My personal debt to Joe is great. I came to Alta a greenhorn, with no sense about anything. He was patient with me and taught me so much that has served me well.

JAMES LAUGHLIN, *Vice President and Director, Alta Lift Co.*

R

REXROTH, KENNETH

Kenneth Rexroth knew everything and would tell you about it.
He had a photographic memory. After lunch he would lie in
his bathtub for two hours, doing some light reading like the
history of Chinese science.

REXROTH

The clarity of the stars seen through tent flaps. Rexroth and I often went camping in the Sierras. As we walked along he would explain all the flora and the geology. He was the best camp cook I ever knew; he could make delicious meals out of things that were light to pack. The master of tomato paste. He always took short pack rods. He could see a trout under the water thirty feet away. He knew the names of all the stars and the myths that

REXROTH IN
THE SIERRAS

went with them. One of our best trips was in late spring but there was still plenty of snow. We climbed in on skis from Bishop on the eastern slope. We camped near a frozen lake. He dug a berth in a snowbank with a ski end and bedded it with fir boughs. He really didn't care much about skiing. He just liked to be in the mountains. Next day I climbed up a big ridge, but he sat all day on a stump—it was sunny—meditating. I looked back down at him every now and then and he never changed his position for three hours.

One year we made the mistake of taking girls along, up King's River Canyon. He brought a poesy-loving coed from San Francisco State and I brought Henry Miller's crazy friend Elena, the one that her husband came home early one day from the office and found us together in the shower; he was so sophisticated, or perhaps he was used to her, he just said: "It is a hot day, isn't it?" To go back: taking the girls was an error. We took a burro that trip to pack the grub and tents and sleeping bags, but the city girls got sore feet and were miserable. Also they didn't like each other. By the time we came down nobody was speaking.

Kenneth sure had a messed up life. A wonder he accomplished as much as he did.

Once he took me to a fancy lunch with some of his rich Jewish friends on Pacific Heights. The hostess asked me, "Don't you think Kenneth burns with too bright a flame?" Sure enough.

REXROTH

*Did you ever know Rexroth? I'm temporarily stuck on doing
his segment [of "Byways"] because he was, in certain cases,
such an awful person. And similarly, on Dylan Thomas, you
can't just write every third line that he was drunk again.
I must find solutions. Actually, Rexroth had a very sweet side
to him, at least he did for me, but he could be so awful to some
of his friends, not to mention strangers . . . Just leave the
[bad stories] out, I guess, and concentrate on our trips in the
Sierras. But it does upset me that Kenneth's books, except for
the oriental translations, sell hardly at all these days.*

*Oh yes, but he told me about some good people. He put me onto
Gary Snyder, a wonderful poet. To Denise Levertov, who is a
marvelous poet and to a couple of others who are first-rate.
He had critical judgment.*

REXROTH

EARLY BACKGROUND

Born 1905. Perhaps in South Bend. Check that Mother was
Delia. Father was Charles. Gambler, alcoholic, Socialist. In and
out of drugstore businesses. 1911, Charles took family to Europe
on biz. Started KR's fix on Europe. Grandfather George Reed.
Called himself an anarchist and was a friend of Eugene Debs.
Sat on porch in stocking feet with Debs drinking whiskey. KR
thought he had some Indian blood. Great-grandmother was
a feminist. KR says she was the first open Lesbian in mid-west.

REXROTH

Dear Delmore,

I really think Rexroth is one of the most superior humans alive. He reminds me extensively of Wheelwright—a Wheelwright without psychic kinks. R. seems to enjoy life. A vast store of anecdotes delivered in an intermountain drawl. We spent Easter rock climbing down in the mountains and you have no idea how near you were to coming into your small fortune. We did a small, very vertical chimney and on the way down my extremities became completely dissociated from the petrous substance. Fortunately the sovietic bard was belaying me with his rope from above and by intellectual ruggedness maintained me in the air, for all the world as Virgil, to whom my poetry has so often been compared, would say, like the wily spider dangling from his self-begotten silky cord, until I retrenched myself in the rock.

READINGS

My pal at BTJ has sent down the video-film of my reading there. If I had known I was being shot I would have tried to be more resolute. The reader is a pathetic old cripple who has to be helped to his chair at the microphone. His tremor is bad and he drops his pages on the floor; but a nubile young maiden rushes up to pick them up for him. He sighs a good deal and when reading "The Inn at Kirchsteten" has to wipe his eyes from emotion. The best part is when he's reading those hot versions of the *Greek Anthology*; the camera pans around the audience and young ladies can clearly be seen rubbing their legs together. *Où sont les neiges . . .*

READING

"What do you read,
    my lord?" asked Polonius.
"Words, words, words!"
    answers Hamlet.

BORIS DE RACHEWILTZ

If it weren't family I'd urge you to do a *New Yorker* profile of
Boris – if anybody would believe him. Henry (at eight) thought
Boris was going to mummify him and ran screaming away. Did
you ever see B's folio prospectus for selling knighthoods in his
order? He offered me a cut rate.

Mary writes that Boris has now
moved from jail to a "clinic."
Is he trying Ezra's stratagem?
Poor Mary.

Did I tell you she made the
cross over me when I put her
on the train at Zell-am-See?

RODITI

I'm working now on a German segment, about the trip Edouard
Roditi and I made in a borrowed army car the year the war had
just ended, inspecting the ruins. But, I've had to change
Edouard's name to Herbert Blechsteiner because I tell about
what he was doing—buying up stolen art works from GI's and
smuggling then out of the country. I also tell about his gay boy
friends, Alexander Koval and Max Faber.

RAPALLO

So when after a few days, not hours, of attentive listening to Pound's polymath monologues which embraced all literatures and history I was invited to enroll sans tuition in the famous "Ezuversity," he found me a room in the apartment of his friend "Ma" Riess at about a dollar a day and tutelage in Italian with the octogenarian Signorina Canessa who hated Il Duce because he had put a tax on canaries.

"Ma" Riess ate early but sometimes she would sit with me while I had my breakfast. She would tell me about her earlier life. She was English, from a middle-class family in Yorkshire, but she had met and married a German businessman from Weimar. Her husband, Max, had prospered.

They had come first to Rapallo on vacation.

When Max died she sold the house in Weimar and moved to Rapallo for the climate. There was a photograph of Max, a good-looking man with a Kaiser Wilhelm mustache, on the wall of her parlor. I also remember color prints of Weimar in Goethe's time and a reproduction of Durer's woodcut of St. Jerome and the lion. And a faded needlework Max's sister had done that said "Immer Gott mit uns" in Gothic script.

She was a Protestant and went to the Anglican church in Rapallo.

What I liked best was when she recited poems of Goethe she had learned in Weimar. I had had a term of German at Harvard but didn't really understand much. She would recite and then paraphrase for me in English. I can still recall some of her favorite lines of Goethe. *"Edel sei der Mensch, hilfreich und gut."* (Let man be noble, helpful and good). I wish I could have modeled my life on that but I am base clay and use people.

ROSTAND

The Rostand and the Peguy
are so ghastly bad I wonder
how you had the stamina
to type them out.

RAPALLO

MUSSOLINI VISITS

RATI-RAHASYAM

O beloved seed of the sacred pomegranate, the chosen food of Sarsawati, I pray that you are not straying from the dhamma pada to meditate on matters such as these:

KOKKOKA THE
RATI-RAHASYAM
16TH CENTURY

"The woman of *kapha* temperament has love and respect for her lover, a soft heart, pearl-like teeth, a skin pale, with the pallor of pining love, and a *yoni* brimful of love-fluid which overflows at the mere touch of her lover.

"The woman of *pitta* temperament has a skin of gold colour, her sweat has an aloetic odour, her temper is neither wild nor mild, has a taste for cold things, and a *yoni* which is always in heat.

"The woman of *vata* temperament has a dark skin, violent temper, vagabond nature, voracious appetite, and a *yoni* rough like the tongue of a buffalo.

"The *kapha* woman is inclined to dream of lotus pools, the *pitta* woman is inclined to dream of blazing fires, and the *vata* woman is inclined to dream of aerial flights."

RUSHDIE

The Rushdie business just makes me feel despondent. Consider that millions of Islamites think the Ayatolah is a hero? Fortunately Rushdie's wife is very beautiful. (Her picture was in the *Times.*) But can she cook well and is she good at checkers? They'll be seeing a lot of each other. I suspect they are stashed away in the Shetlands. I don't think I'll read the book.

READER'S RESPONSES

Dear Mr. Laughlin,

Did you ever question the wisdom of writing a certain letter? Well, I have debated about writing this letter, at least, a dozen times and have, finally, decided to do so.

In the first place, I wouldn't be writing this if I didn't think you had an excellent essay about Kenneth Rexroth in the December issue of **Poetry Pilot.** *However, I believe the line: "than anyone except Ezra Pound—who, by the way, Kenneth detested" is grammatically incorrect. I think it should be: "than anyone except Ezra Pound—whom, by the way, Kenneth detested" since* whom *is the object of the verb detest (namely, Ezra Pound). I am assuming that there is a possibility that you are keeping your literary work for a future book (or, whatever) so it would be important to have it correct.*

However, otherwise, it is one of the most beautifully written literary articles I have ever read . . . in fact, I must confess, for two of the words I had to resort to the dictionary and, may I add, they were used correctly.

Hoping to see more of your writings in the future, I am

Sincerely yours,
Martha Noland Talbert

SMITH, STEVIE

You mention Stevie Smith. She was a doll. I wonder if I have enough "plot" on her (and the famous Aunt) for *Byways*. I wish I could have been present when she went to Buckingham Palace to receive her "damehood." She and the Aunt made her dress themselves. Did you see the film? It was very true to the way they were.

SATANISM

Le dicionnaire infernale, Paris, 1847, might be worth your translating. Satanism is rampant. See article in *New Yawper* about a small town out west where the whole police force buggered their daughters and blamed Satan.

SEMIOTICS

But do tell me what "ism" you profess. Or may I label you a "boa deconstructor"? I'd like that. My style.

SCHWARTZ, DELMORE

Wasn't Delmore wonderful? This shows where some of my funny tone comes from (though also Perelman and Dudley Fitts) but Delmore was six times better. Reading his letters makes me guffaw and weep—the end of his life was so ghastly. Going through the book you can watch him fall apart.

Of course I didn't let the editor of the collection see the really great personal and fantasy letters Delmore wrote me, because one day Delmore came into the office and sorted the letters and sealed the best ones in an envelope marked "Not to be opened until both of us are dead." Note that he didn't want to destroy them.

These letters relate the most extraordinary "facts" about the lives of most of the famous writers we knew. When they are finally published, the whole intimate history of literature in our period will have to be re-written. Some of the greatest are about the love life of Parson Eliot & Vivienne. This was constantly on Delmore's mind, even more than the Giants. I like best the one about what happened in the punt under the bridge at Maidenhead (sic)-on-Thames.

Bellow was writing about Delmore Schwartz in *Humboldt's Gift*. It's a very accurate portrait. Delmore was always inventing fantastic schemes. . . . Hutchins is called "Longseth". . . . And I was called "my playboy publisher."

That came out of the fact that once Delmore sent a manuscript to me to me at Alta which got lost in the bottom of the mailman's truck coming up the canyon. It was some time before it was recovered. Delmore was very agitated. He said that I would have to decide whether I was going to be "a playboy or a publisher."

SWISS SCHOOL

THE DAY IT ALL BEGAN TO FALL APART

It is 1929 and I'm thirteen years old. My school is having a race with another school on Lake Geneva. Our boat is ahead. But I get excited and pull too hard. I catch my pants in the roller of the seat and tip the boat over trying to get free. All in the water. Failure. Disgrace. I'm fired from the crew and am the laughing stock of the school. Everything has been downhill since then.

Friedrich Wilhelm is a ringer for the most hateful master in my Swiss School. Monsieur Laroux taught Latin. He had been ejected from a monastery. I had to sit at his table in the *salle à manger*. He read his *Journal de Lausanne* throughout the meal. If he heard any ruckus at table he would bellow "*un franc d'amende pour tout le monde.*" Our allowance was only three francs a week, which we spent at the confiserie in Rolle, so it was a bitter loss. Monsieur Laroux knew that every modern invention had been invented by Swiss scientists. No doubt about it: airplanes, radio, the works. My life in the *salle à manger* was miserable. A detestable Egyptian named Habibe Sursock sat opposite me, and we weren't allowed to change places. Habibe was

constantly teasing me and kicking me under the table. The dietician believed that the best thing for boys to eat was bread (without butter) and raw radishes. There's more about that lovable institution in the piece "*Salle d'Etude*" in my storybook. I was so unhappy that I studied pretty hard and learned some French.

Le Rosey, near Geneva, was quite a culture shock. There were students from twenty-two countries, including Pahlevi, as we called him, the heir to the throne of Iran. Not a lovable fellow. All he cared about was ice hockey, and we were jealous of his royal privileges; Saturday nights his bodyguards would drive him off to Geneva for amusement.

SELF-DEPRECATION

Plutarch would have no use for me. I've developed a tone of self-deprecation which is blatantly arrogant It doesn't fool anybody. Once in the post office I heard the man clerk, fat Bob, saying to Randy, the girl clerk, "He's pretty stuck on himself, isn't he?" But they've always liked me since the day I was coming in with my arms loaded with packages so I couldn't reach out my hands, and I hadn't tightened my belt properly, so my pants fell all the way down to my ankles.

SITWELL, EDITH

The Seat of the Sitwells is Renishaw Hall. It is in the Midlands coal district and was rather spooky because one could hear the miners' blasting in the depths under the castle all night. It is also the only place where I was treated to a traditional hipper-sponge. Little maids would pop in each morning carrying small buckets of hot water. I would sit on the rim of this ancestral vessel soaping myself. Sit alone unfortunately.

You'll be surprised to learn where I got my slight education in Whitman. It was from Edith Sitwell once when I was visiting her at Renishaw. It turned out that Walt was one of her favorite poets. She read him to me for several hours. The mix of her accent with his tone was rather bizarre. . . . I owe more to Dame Edith than just Whitman. She told me of an astounding young poet whom I would find in a certain pub near Red Lion Square. It was Dylan Thomas.

I had discovered some books of Edith's poetry in the Poetry Room of the Harvard Library and had written her an ardent fan letter. I didn't expect any reply from such an eminent person but within two weeks there was a letter from Renishaw Hall. It was friendly, even chatty, with questions about the new American poets. Which of them would I recommend? I suspected that she might like the Boston poet John Wheelwright whose originality bordered on the eccentric. I sent her his *Rock and Shell*. But it wasn't her dish. Nor did she care for Cummings. Pound turned out to be our link. Early on, she had published an essay on Pound's technique in Canto IV which did much to soften up the British academics on the poem. I learned that one of Edith's favorite poets was Walt Whitman. At that time I had not read enough Whitman to know how good he was. With the arrogance of the ignorant I ventured to argue with her. Something I wrote nettled her and she put me down as I deserved. Parts of her stricture are worth quoting:

"If you want to be a success as editor and publisher, do not write this kind of letter to very eminent people.

Do you play the game Truth? Though I have never met friends of yours, I have heard a good deal about you lately; and I shall not give you 100 points for savoir faire."

Alas, I never made carbons of my letters in those days. I must have mollified Edith because her next letter read:

"I was pretty mad with you—owing, I may say, to something which was entirely your fault. But I couldn't possibly go on being angry with somebody who wrote me this last letter. Anyway, I got you entirely wrong . . . "

And she sent me a packet of her recent books.

STREEP, MERYL

I am in a state of religious exaltation having just seen the Goddess Meryl Streep who is filming in our street. She recognized me as her devotee and smiled at me.

SAINT-SIMON

THE DUC DE SAINT-SIMON
Historical Memoirs

At Versailles only the Queen may have pompons on her coach-covers; fastened with nails, and of any colour that she pleases. Duchesses have blue covers. Wives of eldest sons of dukes have red covers. Widows have black velvet.

I have been having a happy time reading Saint-Simon (the Versailles one). He's a bit self-virtuous but he sure can spin the stories. And those nice wars that began June 1st and halted October 1st and you took 20 servants to the front. What a culture. Is there a good short book about Madame de Maintenon? What was her hold? Did she do dirty things or was she his Mom?

Of Spiced Apples And Relaxation

THE aroma of spiced apples, researchers at Yale University discovered, has a calming effect on many people that tends to lower blood pressure.

In reporting this last spring, Dr. Gary Schwartz, director of Yale's Psychophysiology Center, said the university and the company that financed the research — International Flavors and Fragrances Inc. of Union Beach, N.J. — had applied for a patent on a formulation containing the spiced-apple scent.

Dr. Craig Warren, a vice president and director of organoleptic research for the company, said at the time, "We think that certain smells can make people feel better."

There has been no word yet on the patent application, but the research continues, Dr. Warren reports.

"We've learned a lot about methodology — the technique used to measure the effect on humans," he says, "but not an awful lot about which fragrance does what."

Present studies, he notes, are trying to "extend the applications to a broader screen of moods."

"We're very much interested," he says, "in finding out if a fragrance has some alerting qualities and whether it is arousing — and this would be sexual."

Dr. Schwartz has suggested that aromas might help treat such symptoms as hypertension, headaches, phobias and irritability.

THE NEW YORK TIMES,

JANUARY 26, 1985

SALZBURG JET SET

SALZBURG, DEN
8.25.34

A most amazing day in all. Breakfast in the little garden of the Goldene Rose with Ted Spencer and then to the baths for an hour of sun, where I was eyed most lecherously by several recumbent gents. At the Verkehrbureau I found two delightful letters, one from Father, raising my allowance, God bless him, and another from Fitzgerald, beautiful and casual and inspired as ever. Apertifs at the Bazaar with a mob of people and later lunch at Peterstiftkellar with the same. My new passion with the bangs, Olivia Chambers with the distant ogreous husband at bullfights: the Spencers & an Oxford Don and wife who had been with them at Finstergrün, the wife a most remarkable piece of goods, all gargling and raucous and caustically pretty; the very sedate Forbes of Boston, than which none more, who came from taking the cure at Bad Gastein – the father a perfect piece looking rather like LOBSTOWE, one of those terribly dignified little Bostonians, connected with Cabot, Cabot & Forbes on Milk Street, and garbed in expensive German cameras. Also two daughters, typically Bostonian, cold as icicles, rather pretty, rather cultured, but wholly without spontaneity or any possible *raison d'être* except to be Boston girls. Add to these an amazing little gnat of a man in peasant shorts and a bicycle with an American flag, who had attached himself to Olivia, a chitchat society correspondent, whom one sees dashing about Salzburg, taking pictures of Natasha Pailly Lelong and writing about her new hair dye and tin nipples. After lunch I took black coffee with Gräfin Rümerskirche at her flat, where were Baron and Baronin Engel from Vienna, who knew the Rosey crowd, Franz Colloredo and Dicki Trautenburg, and had been entertained by Aunt Edith and the Stotesburys in Palm Beach. Both terribly finished and stiff. Also Manzi, the Polish soprano, for seven years with the Metropolitan, who is to do the last Isolde here, and her round bald German businessman husband. A terribly impressive woman, warm and strong and sure. Add to these a Baronin Doebelov, who seems to have known the Chandlers, and a Mrs.

McCairn from New York, who has promised me letters to the Viennese ambassador to Budapest. A most interesting piece with her rather horrid daughter. Apparently rich, well-dressed and jewels, a fading blonde with real brains; one conceives of a divorced husband and the desire to raise daughter in Europe and catch a count. Daughter resembling utterly a North Cambridge chippy of the better sort, speaking not much better than one, but knowing all the proper cultural tags, and having an aggressive but effective social technic. Thence to the tea concert at the regal Hotel del'europe for which the Gräfin had given me a bid, where I encountered more lightly worn Austrian swells, a nice little Frenchman who has just done a life of Mozart who said that he liked to "hear music at a distance, but ladies close to hand," and then buried his mustaches in his tea . . .

Afterwards we concluded with a visit to the ChiemSee, which saddened T Sp. for as he said later, he had once been terribly impassioned of a man, and it called back to him that period of spiritual trouble, Olivia insisted that one should ignore such things, and the Baron claimed that only second-rate artists went in for it, which I doubt indeed. Ted was really terribly moved and spoke to me with barriers down as we came home to the Goldene Rose in the late night munching a hot dog. He said "I wish, Jay, that you had somebody in bed with you, either man or woman," to which I replied "that I had for some time had God in bed with me."

SALZBURG

Today it rains (Thursday) so I have been able to break an engagement for swimming with an English girl who isn't very nice anyway, that is to say she is nice, but very English, and so maybe I finish this business now, as I have mentioned almost all the people who are sufficiently interesting to talk about, the others being more or less ordinary.

To me perhaps the most fascinating case in Salzburg is that of an American lady named Mrs. Magrane. I could write a whole book about this lady, for I have listened to her ramble on for almost ten hours at various times, I should think both out of pity and of interest for she includes in herself so very many interesting phenonema. First of all she represents the good mind that has always been grasping for truth and knowledge but has never been disciplined and rendered futile. She knows the most amazing and obscure things but they are all jumbled in her mind and inextricably tangled up with emotional events in her past. Yesterday she told me "You know Milton knew that airplanes would be invented because when you read the passage in *Paradise Regained* where the angels ascend to heaven you find reproduced the exact rhythm of airplane propellors." That is a very representative statement. It represents a mind that is somewhere in the borderlands of fantasy. She has read widely and thought deeply and is always just the least little bit askew. One moment she is talking Steiner and Anthroposophy; the next you would think you were listening to Mrs. Ottarson in a tipsy state; next she is telling your horoscope or reading your palm; then she will be off on her social triumphs, or how she tried to tell President Roosevelt how to manage the currency but he wouldn't believe her. And the fascinating thing is that she actually knows what she's talking about in each field, only when she tries to blend them together they become hopelessly mad. Never have I seen such a thing.

SPERM

I remember the afternoon when E.P. explained the mysteries to me. We were walking up the salita to visit Buttercup & Bismuth (the Drummonds). He said that the epopte was the orgasm, and that the sperm went up to his brain, which was what made him so smart. And Plutarch has some good notes on what went on in that cellar.

SAPPHO

Any notion what endometriosis is?

   Rexroth says Sappho probably had it in a poem I want to use in my next reading and I can't find it in any of my lexicons. Wonder if he made it up? These autodidacts . . .

SEBALD

I'll be interested to have your reaction to *The Emigrants* when you read it. I think it's one of the most beautiful pieces of writing which we have ever published . . . We've never had such good reviews and so many of them on any book in the long history of New Directions. It's a masterpiece if ever there was one.

SEX

IN THE SANSKRIT of the Kama Sutra the rear entrance is referred to as the chuta or mango but around 1935 when I reached Paris it was (at least in the feminine) the *arrière-train.*

SYPHILIS

DR. WIESEL,
JL'S
PSYCHIATRIST

JL,

Query – You must have known that 606 [JL's post office box number in Norfolk] was the number given to the first successful drug to treat syphilis! You wicked man!

BW

Dear BW,

I hope you are feeling ever so much better now. I await your invitation to come in.

I stopped the Prozac a few days ago because it was projecting me like a missile up into the clouds. I fear a natural mania has taken over. But I haven't murdered anybody. The Prozac wakes me up at 3 AM and makes me write seditious poems. I'll enclose samples so you can study my case.

I didn't explain why at the Post Office, but I've gotten them to put me on the waiting list for a less insinuating number.

SAROYAN

I'm sorry but I can't let you have proofs on the stories.

By sad experience I have had to make that the rule.

If I let every contributor have proofs it would cost me

$150 in corrections. You don't know what authors are like

because you are one. First, authors don't know that

corrections cost $3.50 an hour, secondly they don't realize

that when they change one word in linotype it knocks

out a whole page of slugs and that costs two or three hours'

time to fix.

    Thirdly, authors just have to take one look at a page of

proofs to go entirely crazy and decide they are Jesus instead

of Napoleon and rewrite the damn thing.

    I'm sorry, I just can't afford it. You authors will have to realize

that we small publishers can print you but can't humor you . . .

    College keeps me working like a shithouse eel.

No time for letters.

LETTER
TO WILLIAM
SAROYAN
10.11.37

SKIING

And it all began, the whole life of skiing, when a friend of my mother's, a Scottish lady who was actually a golf champion, left in our attic a pair of clumsy old skis that had no bindings, just a leather loop where you put your foot. My brother and I took them to a steep hill by the college and started sliding, but mostly falling, having no idea what we were doing. Then some years later we were put in a fashionable school (Le Rosey) in Switzerland, where skis by then had primitive clasp bindings so we learned a bit about turning. No ski-lifts yet in the Bernese Oberland. We packed our skis on our shoulders up the mountain, which was called the Windspielen, meaning the playground of the winds.

SKIING

Skiing weekends from Harvard were winter routines. We could drive to Stowe, Vermont, in about six hours, or to Mount Washington in five. There were no ski-lifts in those days, We hiked up the mountains with sealskins or carrying our skis. A bed in a tourist home only cost a few dollars. A big breakfast in a village restaurant might be less than a dollar. Or, if it wasn't blizzarding, there was the Harvard Mountaineering Club hut at the base of Tuckerman's Ravine on Mt. Washington. A two-hour hike packing some grub and a sleeping bag. We had informal races among different college teams on the narrow tree-lined tracks. Too narrow for me. I swung a turn too wide and smashed into a tree, shearing off some processes on my spine. It hurt like all hell and I hollered accordingly. The rescue toboggan was hauled up for me, a kindly ranger gave me a shot, and I woke up in the Conway Hospital. My father was, of course, in a fit. He had me transported by ambulance to Brooks Hospital in Boston. Where an eminent orthopedics specialist swaddled me in an enormous cast and kept me in it for two months. The effect of this treatment was to permanently weaken the musculature of my back. I've had a bad back ever since. Today they would have had me up and walking in a week. But I've never stopped skiing.

I don't want this snow-
light to end.
I'd like to stretch it out endlessly.

SKIING

THE ADVENTURES OF ST. ANTON

That was where I had my pants sewn up by the Queen of Holland. A group of us out on a tour. I fell and put a big rip in the butt of my hosen; but her majesty had a sewing kit in her sitzpack and quickly repaired me. Then there was the promising young conductor from Vienna, Herbert von Karajan, a fine and fearless skier. He took pity on my shortage of cash for the busses. He would ride me up the mountain in his chauffeured car then let me ski down with him, coached by his private instructor, Luggi Foerger. That year the girls of the American ski team were training in St Anton. A fetching bunch of mostly society girls; for them the big thing was the tea dances in the fancy Hotel Post.

GREAT MOMENTS IN THE INTELLECTUAL HISTORY OF EUROPE.

HRH KONINGIN WILHELMINA OF THE NETHERLANDS READING EZRA POUND'S TRANSLATION OF CONFUCIUS, THE GIFT OF HEER JAAP LAUGHLIN, WHOSE SPLIT TROUSERS SHE ONCE REPAIRED WITH THE ROYAL SEWING KIT ON A SKI SLOPE OF THE ALPS.

DRAWING BY
GUY DAVENPORT
2.8.86

SWAN, LILY

I fell just a little bit in love with
Lily Swan, who later married a
famous architect, but was too
shy to do much about it.

SPENCER, TED

Ted Spencer was my favorite professor at Harvard. He was also 1939 the favorite of the Radcliffe students including my wife who had him ten years later; she still raves about his manly charm. He was tall, blonde and very handsome, a self-deprecating aristocrat. He had been to varsity in England; there was a pleasant tinge of "U" in his accent. A knight from the field of Agincourt but his weapon was humor. The seminar that I took with him on Joyce, Mann and Proust was enthralling. Best of all, he never expected us to read all those long texts. Scene after scene we received all the high spots and best passages in his witty and elegant utterance. Ted had written his first books on Shakespeare, which led to his job at Harvard; then he turned to the moderns. His interest in me clearly came from what I could tell him about Pound. Soon he was inviting me to play tennis and to meals at his house. Finding that his wife was much concerned about the state of the world, I converted her—much to Ted's amusement—to Pound's doctrines of Social Credit. She even joined the Boston Social Credit party, which was headed by an equally high-minded lady on Beacon Hill, Mrs. E. Sohier Welch. There were tea parties of intense indignation in a Jamesian setting. But few converts. Too many of Mrs. Welch's friends were the wives of plutocrats. It was wind in a bucket. Boston was firmly in the grip of bankers and lawyers whose management of the economy was acknowledged to be perfect. I was a bit more militant; one day I was ejected from the Boston Mass Transit for distributing handbills to the downtrodden. When Pound returned from Italy to the States in 1939 he headed first to Boston. He wanted to consult on strategy for ridding the country of usurious banks with Congressman George Holden Tinkham with whom he had been corresponding about monetary crime. Ezra had great hopes for the legendary Tinkham, a Brahmin who once while campaigning had made headlines by riding his horse into a bar in Roxbury. Such a man obviously had the flair to publicize Social Credit to the electorate.

When I told Spencer that Pound was coming to Boston Ted invited him to be his houseguest. The week of Pound's visit in Oxford Street was certainly the most colorful that the Spencer household ever experienced. Wyndham Lewis had christened Ezra the "Pantechnikon" for his entrepreneurial energy. Joyce described him as a "bundle of unpredictable electricity." Add Pound's ever-darting lively eyes and the foxy charm.

There was another regrettable event, at least for Ted. Ted fancied his artistry on the tennis court, but Ezra trounced him in doubles. Ezra's tennis was based on force not speed. He would position himself at half-court, scowling fiercely at his opponents, and wait to unleash a powerful full-body-pivot forehand which was quite unreturnable.

STEIN

It has been very nice to know Miss Stein and also it has
its drawbacks. Each time you know a great person you begin
to know more and more that you yourself are not a great
person and that it would be much more sensible not to live in
Pittsburgh and work in the steel mill and marry a nice plain
girl who can't read Bach and has a turned up nose. You begin
to see that it was natural for you to think for awhile that you
were a great person, because it is this which is the best thing
about living, this thinking and wanting to think that you are
better than you are and wanting to be that, but that really it
was just thinking and not much more.

However, I am not discouraged, though greatly reduced.
At present I wouldn't lay much money on my literary success,
because I'm beginning to see what writing really is and that
it is not what I thought it was but really I wouldn't as yet lay
much money against my still trying to write because really
there is only one thing that pleases and that is knowing and
when you are writing and trying to write you are knowing
things and trying to tell what you know and tell what it is best
to know. You see that don't you; yes of course anybody can
see that.

with love J

I shan't mail this for a while as a letter costs ten cents
in this country and that is a lot of money I can tell you.

Dear Mother and Father,

*Well tomorrow morning I am setting off for Paris and very sorry
I shall be indeed to leave this lovely place and kind people. I hope
Mama will write, as she always does, a nice letter to Miss Stein
to thank her for being so good to me. (27 Rue de Fleurus, Paris is
the right address.) And if you hear that she is going to lecture in
Pittsburgh be sure to have her at the house, because she has
always lived in her own place and can't bear the thought of
having to go to hotels during her lecture tour.*

*Bernard Fay is going to drive me as far as Cosne tomorrow
where I shall get an express for Paris, landing there in the late
night. So I shan't join Mlle until the next morning.*

*Since I have been here I have done most and best the changing
of tires. Every day when we go riding a tire goes flat and
sometimes twice, and then I change them. Miss Stein is very
glad to have me along to change them because usually she just
waits until someone comes along on a bicycle and does it for her.
I told her how good you were at changing tires and she said she
certainly hoped she would see you. If you see her you must talk
about her dogs; she will talk about them all the time and likes it.
They get washed and brushed and polished every day and are
handfed. You should see how funny they are together, the big
white poodle Basket and the lively little black Pepi. If you pat
Basket, Pepi will come and nip you; and if you pick up Pepi,
Basket will begin to cry and he can really cry. The other night
we had dinner at a famous restaurant in Belley, and while we sat
there for two hours Basket never once took his eyes off the door
where Miss Stein had gone in; we could see him doing this from
the window.*

STEIN

I like Gertrude Stein very well and she is a great woman but one
can never be sure. She knows more about writing and words than
anyone else has ever known surely and yet sometimes I think
there are things we live which a word cannot tell even when, as
in her writing, you give it not its name but the word that makes
it be without repeating it. She is very nice to me and very frank;
she is the most frank person I have ever known. There is no
waste material about her at all, and she has a smile in her eyes
that is second only to Whitehead's. I have learned more about
writing in these few days than ever I have known before . . .

After lunch we go driving in the Ford. Miss Stein fills the car
quite completely though she is not big, but she is like a rock sit-
ting there quite solidly, and she holds the wheel still after driving
for thirty years as though it were something she did not quite
trust. She drives very fast and very well and never looks at the
road but is never in the wrong place. Some days we go to see
a church, one day we went to see a Roman column, today we
went swimming in the Lac de Bourget and yesterday we went
to Aix. In the evening we sit and talk and everyone tells stories
about people and places and things. It is very nice. I sleep very
well and have no dreams. I cannot tell you about Basket and Pepi
because I am not very good at dogs, but they are quite
as important as anyone else.

BILIGNIN,
BELLEY AIX
7.9.34

NEW DIRECTIONS
Publishing Corporation

333 Sixth Avenue
New York City 10014

STEIN

"Extremely useful,"
Gertrude Stein said of him
when he was 19.

Gertrude Stein was the most
charismatic pyramid ever built.

STELOFF, FRANCES

One of our great culture heroes: Miss Frances Steloff of the Gotham Book Mart on 47th Street. The first orders I received for Pound and Williams came from her . . . she can smell good books, and from a long distance.

Not lacking in brashness, to get his venture underway, he wrote to tell all the avant-garde writers whose work he admired, asking for pieces to print. All but six of them complied though there was no mention of payment. The contents list included: Elizabeth Bishop, Kay Boyle, Jean Cocteau, e.e. cummings, Eugene Jolas, Henry Miller, Marianne Moore, Ezra Pound, Gertrude Stein, Wallace Stevens, William Carlos Williams, and Louis Zukofsky. The fact that the boy publisher forgot to ask the printer to number the pages did not hurt the sale. With the active support of the legendary figure Frances Steloff, proprietor of the Gotham Book Mart on 47th Street, an edition of 600 copies priced at $2 quickly sold out.

STEVENS, WALLACE

Not easy to talk to, not much bubble, a grave counselor. . . . It is said that he composed his poems while walking to and from his house and office. And it is reported that his wife, the lady so beautiful that her head was modeled on the old Liberty dime, did not encourage literary visitors at lunch. He had to take them to the Hartford Canoe Club.

SIDDHARTHA

The longer I publish the less I know what it's about or what makes a book sell. Sometimes the books I think are the best don't sell at all, whereas others that I don't think are so good sell very well. A case in point is Hermann Hesse's *Siddhartha*, which Henry Miller sent my way. Henry was quite a mystic and he loved philosophy; he always said he wanted to die in Tibet. Henry was a dear man but he never made it to Tibet because his Japanese friend spent so much of his money. Now I'm sure he is in some happy place where people as nice as Henry go, though some of his favorite sports may not be available to him in the form which he has now assumed. Anyway, Henry kept writing me about the Hesse book. An English lady, Hilda Rosner, had sent him a translation of *Siddhartha*. I went through it and thought it was very readable, but a little too Germanic and the message just Buddhism with a sugar coating. I stalled but Henry would write about every three months saying I *had* to publish that book. Finally, to oblige Henry, I did. The first year it sold only 400 copies, but sales kept growing and at the height of the Hesse boom we sold a quarter of a million copies in a year.

SIDDHARTHA

HERMANN HESSE

THOMAS, DYLAN

Dear Thomas,

Your letter had quite an effect on me. When I got it in Paris I was just on the point of going batting off to Spain to fight in the War. Then I thought about your situation and that of two other young writers of mine in America and I said God now I can't do that, I've got a duty to do. So I didn't go. I can't get myself killed right now.

As long as you stay good and write the real thing you will never make money. I must tell you that. You must resign yourself to that. That is the state of publishing today. Novels make money. Everything else begs its way. It is against that that I'm fighting. But it's a hell of a fight.

But you can count on me to do what I can for you. At this moment I have almost no money at all, but in good times I have plenty. My money comes from steel shares left in trust for me by my father. The trouble is that I cannot touch the principal or revise the holding. Thus when steel is down I am just as badly off as anybody else.

So I cannot promise you very much right now. I can send you twenty dollars now and the same again next month. If business gets better in America I can do more for you. The important thing is for you to manage to live somehow and go on writing. Your first few books will not make anything, but that doesn't matter. Later on you may make a little. In the meantime I'll do my best to see you through. But I want you to know how things are with me.

New Directions is the best publisher for you in America because I fight for my books. None of the big houses will fight for a poet these days. If they think he'll write a novel they'll play him along, but they won't fight for him as a poet.

Wales sounds fine. I don't know how much time I'll have in London, but I would really like to see you in the country rather

than the city. I hate London. I've always been miserable there,
and I don't imagine it will be much different this time. I wouldn't
come at all except that many things have to be fixed up in
connection with distributing my books in London.

It would be fine if I could come down to Wales to see you for
a weekend. But maybe there won't be time. In any case, let me
know what you do, and keep me posted. You might stir up Reavey
to send along those proofs. And if you have any new work that
isn't in the Baby you might let me see that, as I want something
for the anthology. And I don't think I've seen the second book of
your poems.

I shall be here with Pound for about three weeks I think. He
is a great old character. It is rather annoying that he has turned
to fascism. It is so inconsistent with his early writing. But I
manage to separate politics from poetry and personality and
we get along first rate. I was here with him twice before, once
for nearly a year. Rapallo is a great place—hills coming right
down into the sea, lovely old town with a million stinks in it,
and the Italian fecundity and exuberance of life. Many places
in America you wouldn't know the planet was inhabited. Here
the whole air breathes with centuries of life and death—not
that there are monuments about, but just that the people look
so damn permanent and there are so many
of them in such a small space.

Well, see you soon, and let me hear from you.

Laughlin

Sometimes these parties went on all night, and we found ourselves waking up in the apartment of some stranger we didn't even know. Once it was Edouard Roditi's mother, who sobered us up with a crashing breakfast of ham and eggs.

. . . he drank them all off, passed out and was carted off to St. Vincent's in an ambulance. What his death certificate reads is "insult to the brain."

Someone had to go over to the morgue to identify the body, because Dylan was a foreign citizen who had died under unusual circumstances. So John Brinnin—the promoter of his American tours—and I tossed a coin. I lost, so I went. The morgue was part of Bellevue Hospital—not the beautiful new place that's there now where they put the bodies, and you go in and there's lovely muzak. Back then, it was an awful place, smelling of formaldehyde. There was this little old guy trundling corpses around on gurneys. He would pull a rubber sheet back and ask, "Is this him?" "No." "Is this him?" "No." Finally we found him. He looked awful, all puffy and purple. "Yeah, that's him." And he said, "Well, you go over there to the window, and identify him." In the window was a little girl. She was about four feet high, and I don't think she had even finished high school yet. She filled out the forms—she couldn't spell Dylan so I spelled it out for her. "What was his profession?" "He was a poet." That puzzled her. This little girl said, "What's a poet?" "He wrote poetry." So that is what the form says: "Dylan Thomas. He wrote poetry."

THOMAS, DYLAN

Dylan wanted to drink every day and all day if possible. This was difficult for a light drinker. One morning Dylan knocked at my door at Claridges and was deeply distressed. He said that his younger brother Llewellyn had come down with tuberculosis and had to go to an expensive sanatorium. It would cost £1000. I took Dylan to the bank and a thousand single pounds were counted out into his hand. (There were no large bills at that time.) What was my chagrin at a party two days later when he laughed over the fact that his brother didn't have the disease after all. He thought it was a very funny joke, but I bore down on him and got him to sign a paper that the £1000 was to apply to the royalties of all the books of his we would later publish at New Directions. He kept is word on that, and it was one of the most valuable business strokes I ever put across.

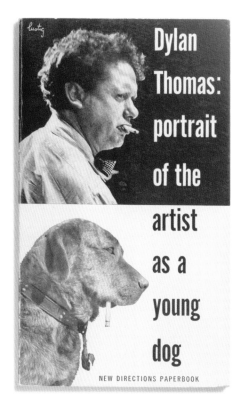

TIME

TIME IS MONEY

All my life I have addressed letters to the metropolis "New York, NY." Now I find from letters forwarded up here that "NYC" is sufficient, they get delivered. Using the stop watch that serves to time my poetry readings, I find that the abbreviation would save me nearly 3 seconds of valuable time. Usually I write about 10 letters a week to NYC. If I suffer through three more years of my life of pain, what will my net gain be?

TORTELLINI

Severi, one of my Italian translators, informs me that the tortellini of Modena, her home place, are modeled on the belly-button of Venus.

THOREAU

Thoreau was our Diogenes . . . MAKE IT NEW first appears in American writing in Walden; Henry was a great Confucian. He was a crack classicist also: translated Anakreon. He was a vegetarian, by the way: no rabbits.

TRANSITION

I learned about *transition* from Gertrude Stein, who published in it, the summer before I went to study with Pound, who thought GS was a nut. The "Revolution of the Word" concept was the gospel of *transition*. I had no connection with Eugene Jolas, the editor of *transition*. I just liked his theories that language must be constantly renewed. Pound had no connection with the *transition* group. His renewals were of a totally different order. *Broom* I never read.

TRANSLATION

In his preface to *Sylvae* Dryden wrote:

Methinks I come like a Malefactor, to make a speech upon the Gallows, and to warn all poets, by my sad example, from the sacrilege of translating Virgil.

All I can answer is that I will ever pray for the translators who may have risked perdition to give me so much pleasure.

THOMAS, CLARENCE

You've missed one of the great soap operas of all time—the hearings of the Senate on Bush's nomination of Clarence Thomas (a mediocrity but he's black). All was moving ahead when a lady who had worked for him came out of the underbrush to accuse him of sexual harassment. She remembered all the dirty things he had told her, and it all went out over the TV. The press went wild. Surely nothing like this ever happened in the Roman Senate, even in the reign of Caligula. He denied everything and got approved. But there has been a nationwide outburst of feminism such as we never had.

TRAVEL

1935   I am going to see Gertrude Stein for a few days on Friday and then I am going to Lausanne—Basel—Freiburg—Strassbourg—Stutgart (H. Baines)—Wurzburg—Erfurt—Leipzig—Dresden—Prague—Brunn—Bratislava—Budapest—Vienna—Linz—Salzburg—Ljubljana—Zagreb—Dubrovnik. What all this will add up to is not known, but if I write one poem in each place, I shall have had some practice in this matter.

U
V

ULYSSES

Joyce has been an overpowering presence in my mind since I was seventeen but I never read *Ulysses* first page to last, every magical word and line, until I was sixty. All those years I read about him, I read the minor works, I talked knowingly about him, I published *Stephen Hero* and reprinted *Exiles*, I brought out Harry Levin's pioneering book on him and Forrest Read's edition of the Pound/Joyce correspondence, I even met him, but I didn't really come to grips with *Ulysses*. I'm afraid this tells a lot about the superficiality of my literary life. A skimmer. A dipper. A plucker. A faker? But perhaps the forty years' procrastination was just as well. If I had tackled *Ulysses* whole at seventeen I would have missed so many of its marvels for want of background. At sixty much, though far from all—who could recognize everything?—was apparent. And still one learns from the text. It becomes more embracing, even of one's own experience. The last line of a crucial poem written at seventy, "Confusio Senectutis," is from the last phrases of *Ulysses*.

UNCLE HARRY

The big storm gave us over two feet of snow, more than I've ever seen here, and the place looks very poetical. But, alas, the wind took down Uncle Harry in the yard, the biggest maple in Norfolk. But Unc was past his time. In 1945, Ole Zetterstrom, the 1928 Olympic champion in the 50-kilometer at Chamonix, spent a month repairing the scar that a lightning bolt (celestial?) had given him. (Uncle Harry was the terror of his generation, making trouble faster than his transgressions could be counted, but lovable about it, you know, lovable.)

VENDLER, HELEN

Dear Guy,

I was touched, deeply touched, by your offer of an introduction. You are too indulgent about my eccentric verses, but you are magical with the words and could even soften the heart of that dreadful woman Harry Levin imported into the Harvard English Department—I dislike her so much I can't remember her name— who is said to control poetry reviewing at both the NYTBR *and* The New Yorker, *bloody woman who wrote a purty good book about Jarge Herbert and then went off the deep end into pure shit (Ezra speaking). Don't know for nuffin about poesy. Didn't put Snyder, Levertov, Oppen, Zuk, or Olson into her buggarin amfollogy, says Ez is "archaeologically of some interest," Christ and a bear as my first father-in-law used to say, what we have to put up with. (Now it comes up: Helen Vendler.)*

VALUES

A SYLLOGISM ON VALUES

A: Laurie reports from the NYC office that that cow Mrs Sinkler
(who edits the *Times Book Review* and has almost entirely removed poetry reviews from its pages) called to say that she
found my "remarks" at the NBA affair so lovely, sic so *lovely*,
could she have a copy to print them . . . and Laurie knew that
was good publicity for selling books. My remarks were not lovely, they were sheer cat-piss . . . excuse me, child of Humphrey,
dog-dirty.

B: Lady Cunard invited Ronald Firbank to lunch at the Ritz. He
studied the menu carefully and ordered one pea. When the sole
pea arrived on a plate, it was cold. It was taken back for warm-
ing. Firbank had *values* and he had class. As you know, when he
went to France he took a small trunk full of English coal. French
coal didn't burn well. Values.

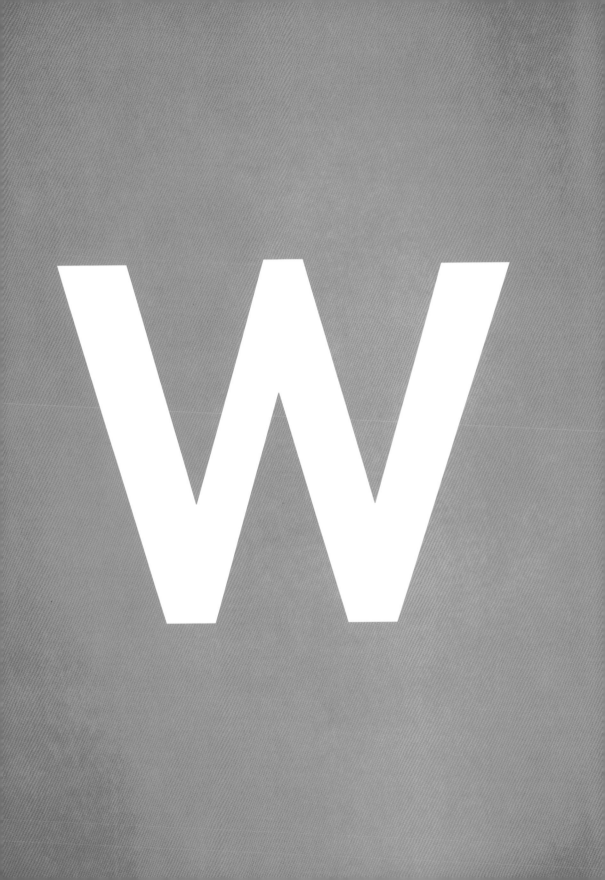

WHEELWRIGHT, JACK

Jack Wheelwright has been with me all day, as amusing and irrational as ever. . . . He says the way to cure his indigestion is to eat a whole box of caramels.

WINTER

A marvel of nature. In the night it rained then turned very cold. In the morning every twig and branch was encased in ice. A world of ice. When we went outside there were a thousand firecrackers going off as branches cracked and split and fell. That went on all day. The road to town was blocked with the debris. The power went off. No sun came out to melt the ice. But at dusk the colors were superb. A soft gray sky. The lighter shades of the softening trees. Here and there a dark green hemlock standing out at the edge of the forest.

WILLIAMS, ROSE

Once there was a revival of *The Glass Menagerie* in New York and we arranged for a car to take her and her nurse to see it. She enjoyed herself watching the stage action without ever realizing that the play was about her. It was all so sad, and that dreadful operation caused it.

Rose was very mute but she didn't seem unhappy. She never spoke of Tennessee, but the nurse said she had a pack of the postcards he had sent her which she would look at now and then. We took her out to dinner. What she wanted was to smoke many cigarettes, drink coca cola and have steak. The nurse said she was very quiet but refused to do the leather work therapy.

WILLIAMS, TENNESSEE

NATIONAL
ARTS CLUB
SPEECH
01.1983

It was James Laughlin in the beginning and it remains James Laughlin now, with never a disruption or moment of misunderstanding in a friendship and professional relationship that has now lasted for forty years or more.

By nature I was meant more for the quieter and purer world of poetry than, for the theatre into which necessity drew me.

And now as a time for reckoning seems near, I know that it is the poetry that distinguishes the writing when it is distinguished, that of the plays and of the stories, yes, that is what I had primarily to offer you.

I am in no position to assess the value of this offering but I do trust that James Laughlin is able to view it without regret. If he can, I cannot imagine a more rewarding accolade.

WIESEL, DOCTOR

BW had long maintained that he could take my mental temperature better by studying my poems than by listening to my hypochondriacal complaints. Once when I sent him a poem from California he cabled to advise that I needed a bit more Etrafan. (There are no different sizes.) Break off half a pill and take it at bedtime. Let me know how that goes in two weeks.

I would never question your scholarly acuity, but
to your ref. 677, note c, of the Tibetan PDR, re fingers, I think
I might prefer the following, which is from the Pali version
of the Dharmalakapu-denda Sutra, Shastra III, Smriti 6-11.

Un so weiter 5 lines, vide **The Harvard Oriental Series,**

Volume 16, Cambridge, 1922, or the perhaps preferable

text of the Biblioteca Indica, Calcutta, 1893.

   Now I must confess that my Pali has slipped since I was

thrown out of Arakan in 1961 by that puritanical sonofabitch

General Ne Win whom I declined to cut in on my rather

profitable little poppy growing operation, but I would say

that these lines could be roughly rendered in the vernacular:

Ipsi dixit, quandocumquigitur videlicet, etc.

Beware the she—cat Demon Padhmaegrunda
If she attempts to introduce her cold finger*
Into your nostril or other orifice
She is not interested in providing gustation
But intends to remove your Third Eye**
Whence you'll lose your tantric vision
Of things past and things to come.

*Well, if red wine is bad for my esaupophagous (I believe that
Adamastor, the physician of the emperor Diocletian, preferred
this sort of transliteration from the Greek) I will trade in my
Clos Vougeot and Haut Brion for a cask of pomegranate juice.
Ah, those tepid afternoons on the lawn of the Willingdon Polo
Club in Bombay, sipping their ichor of pomegranate laced with
brandy distilled from palm wine, where I played on the team
of my Cambridge college mate the Nawab of Marilabad, such
a chukka-pukka spot, no Dravidians allowed past the gate,
and in 1965 we whopped Sir Jehangir Jeejeeboy and his crowd,
despite the money those upstart Parsees had to spend
on Arabian ponies. Ah well . . .*

* The Demon's finger is cold because she is a dead ghost. Ed.
** The spurious and entirely magical "Third Eye" was introduced into Tibetan Tantrism circa 747 AD by the "Great Guru,"
Padhma Sambava, founder of the Nyingmapa sect, who came from South India and corrupted the hardy but superstitious
mountaineers with degenerate practices. Ed.

WOMEN

O TATHÂGATA

You make to quiver the curious nerves of servant by not mentioning the name of the fortunate lady who is said to have described me as "nice." This is a rather broad term, even for a small lady, and I am all ears to know which one. Let us express the hope that she remains cool in the head and warm in the bed. I have never felt that the General Electric Corporation solved the problem of the sexes with the electric blanket. There is more to it than that, though I do not just yet know what.

WRIGHT, FRANK LLOYD

Frank Lloyd Wright was a rather odd sort of man. He loved low ceilings. When Edgar Kaufmann invited me to Falling Water near Pittsburgh, I kept bumping my head. And I always had occipital bruises when I was staying at the Wright-designed Imperial Hotel in Tokyo.

WRITING HABITS

. . . but I guess you've seen enough of my product, which, like defecation, is an almost daily occurrence. But let me know. I suppose Cid Corman is the only one who writes *every* day. I'm sometimes "irregular" as they say in the TV ads.

WEINBERGER, ELIOT

Yes, Eliot is you-knee-cue, but how to put him across in this desert of insensitivity to literary imagination? I can't remember any important reviews of *Works on Paper*. In France he would already be famous. *Traenen und Weh*. And then there is the whole subject of G. Bush. The Republic is foundering.

I'm very grateful to your learning which has given me a broader view of the naked mole-rat.

WCW

I'm sorry you will miss my début as a chantooose. Next week will intone poems of W.C.W. with a woodwind quintet at the Hirschorn in Wash/D.C. Think I had better not explain that "Queen Anne's Lace" is about an orgasm, or that the "yellow stain" is on Bill's bed sheet, not on the flower.

Dixit M. Perloff

WOMEN

LA NANA

Thank you for putting me on to The Pléiade XVIème volume and the lovely quotations from it. I should be able to get the French bookstore in NYC to order that for me. Daniel brought up from Columbia Blasons, Poésies Anciennes, Paris 1809. The verse is elegant but not dirty enough for my needs. And I would like to find some evil engravings or woodcuts.

In a woman or in a poem, unpredictability is the big thing.

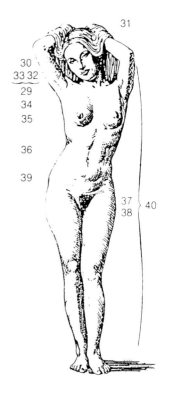

Do you remember Leontina, the girl in the underwater cave in my poem "In Another Country"? She called from Rome today to wish me "Buon Natale," as she does every year, which means, though she doesn't say so, that she needs money for the rent—and I don't let her down. "Ti ricorda, Giacomino, come noi siamo stati ragazzi insieme a Rapallo," she likes to say. Yes, I remember real good. For a while she had it very rough. During the war when there were no jobs and nothing to eat, she had to take up with German officers to survive. But the Krauts didn't corrupt her proud Ligurian spirit. She soon married an extremely nice and bright economic journalist on a Rome paper and they had a good life till he died. But his pension doesn't amount to much now with the inflation. Dorothy Pound didn't approve of her—she was only the daughter of the janitor in the Rapallo bank—but Ezra thought she was very good for me, and he was right.

WITTGENSTEIN

I am curious about Wittgenstein. Any philosopher who could say "You can't catch cold over the telephone" certainly discovered Truth. But he didn't know everything. On our farm we have a fifty-year-old tractor to plough snow that is neurotic. Sometimes one tread runs forward and one goes backwards. If you call the mechanic it's $75. Then it does it again. I consulted our local librarian. She produced a book by Mr. Wittgenstein about Tractors. But the answer was not there. At Brown when I was doing Pound I met the brilliant, German-born poet Rosmarie Waldrop. She thought it was a disgrace to Brown I didn't know about Wittgenstein. She set out to teach me. But her pedagogical method is rather like Ezra's. She begins a stanza with a principle of Wittgenstein's, but the next five lines are not by Wittgenstein but by her. Confusing.

WEEDING

The garden is a riot of multicolored confusion. What I like best is to weed. What does that say?

WILLIAMS, WILLIAM CARLOS

That God damned and I mean God damned poem **Paterson**
has me down. I am burned up to do it but don't quite know how.
I write and destroy, write and destroy. It's all shaped up in
outline and intent, the body of the thinking is finished but the
technique, the manner and the method are unresolvable
to date. I flounder and flunk.

WCW TO JL
1943

I get moments of despair over **Paterson,** *the usual thing, a feeling*
that I'm through for life, just a wash-out. Something lower than
the lowest. Then again I spark along for a few lines and think
I'm a genius. The usual crap. I'll do the best I can.

WCW TO JL
11.1948

Yours of the 9th to hand, and what a magnificent kick in
the teeth that is—administered, I may say, with a touch that is
definitely deft, and almost that one might think, of a practiced
hand at this sort of thing; which, of course, you aren't—the
furthest thing from it—but how easily we drift into
it when the devil has planted the seed.

  Yes, a lovely reward for a decade of work and faith and
sacrifice. More power to you. I love the human race. The more
they try to kick me around the better I love them. Sure thing.

  Frankly, Bill, I would never have dreamt that you, of all
people, would fall this low. I suppose I have always carried
you around on my special idealistic pedestal. You have always
seemed to me the whitest of the white, the real human
being complete with sense and feeling.

JL TO WCW
2.12.50

Well, I am hurt. I am terribly hurt, I won't conceal it, and from zers have told me what faithless bastards writers are I have held you up as an example of loyalty. I feel exactly like Gretchen's brother in Faust. *Look up the passage and read it for me.*

But go your way—with my blessing. You are a loveable cuss, and I'll be sore for a few weeks, but it will pass. What you are doing is only human, and I've done plenty of things myself on a par with it. I can't complain.

Still in all, it's incredible, unbelievable. Have you no insight? Are you totally blind about your work and its nature? Do you really think that you can sell yourself to the masses, no matter how hard you try to write what they want?

All right . . . go to the big boys. They were swell to you about publishing White Mule, *weren't they? They did a beautiful job on the* Collected Poems *didn't they? They fell over themselves didn't they to get a critic to write a book about you? They overwhelmed you, didn't they, with offers to keep the* American Grain *in print? Go to them. Rush. Run. Don't lose a second. Let them slobber their dirt all over your decency and your purity. And offer up to them as a little bribe* my *pride, and* my *life's devotion to an ideal. See how dirty they can make that too.*

Well Bill, I'm sorry to have talked to you this way. It's not respectful, it's not friendly. But you have hurt me deeply and terribly, and the only way to get it out of my system is to talk right out, cauterize it, and then forget it.

You say you need money. Let me remind you that I offered to put you on a monthly check basis, as I do with [Henry] Miller, and you turned it down. I suppose you had your reasons.

WILLIAMS, WILLIAM CARLOS

One day when I arrived at 9 Ridge Road in the late morning I saw an unexpected and encouraging sight. Bill had had a burst of energy and was typing, with one finger, at the dining room table. Floss put her head in from the kitchen to tell me, "Don't disturb him, he's practicing by trying to write me a letter." The floor was littered with balls of paper Bill had crumpled up and thrown away. When he was tired and stopped his work I picked up one of the balls and deciphered it later out in the car. The typing was mostly wrong, but this is what he wanted to say.

Dear Floss,
Thank you for everything.
Forgive me. I always loved you.
Bill

Miraculously, as Bill kept up his practice on the machine he made much improvement so that his letters were easier to understand and Floss could mail them. Here is the last letter to me that he typed himself.

Dear Jim,
I fnally got your letter enclosing your letter enclocussing
your letter which was so ompportant foe me, thannkuok
youn very much. In time this fainful bsiness will will
soonfeul will soon be onert. Tnany anany goodness.
If Slossieeeii wyyonor wy sinfsigna-ture.

I hope I hope I make it
Bill

WILLIAM CARLOS WILLIAMS

Whose Books Are Published by New Directions

WILLIAMS, TENNESSEE

Dear Jay,

*We are passing through Hattiesburg Mississippi en
route to Washington D.C. for the "command performance"
of "Menagerie." I had decided not to go up for it as I have
so fallen in love with N.O.LA that I was unwilling to part
with it for even a week-end, but a young lady friend of
mine thought differently and bought my ticket and poured
me on the train more or less forcibly. She is along too
and that may be why she was firm about it. In fact I am
going through quite an experience with this young lady.
Who is one of these people with a passion for lost causes,
is beautiful enough to have anybody she wanted but is
apparently attracted only by the line of most resistance.
So she came down here from New York and so far the most
complete and graphic candor on my part has not convinced
her that propinquity will not conquer all. I have always
been more or less overlooked by good-looking women and
once upon a time I sometimes suffered acutely from the
fact, so the novelty of the situation makes it all the more
impossible to cope with. I dare say you have had infinitely
more experience in the matter and at any rate are infinitely
more resourceful, so let us exchange fatherly advices. No,
I don't want to be "saved"; I don't think any one has ever
been happier with his external circumstances than I have
learned how to be, and as for my internal circumstances,
only I can affect them. So is there anything to be gained*

from the complicating entrance of a lady? I would like to
arrange for you to meet her, for she is a delectable article
for anyone on the market, or are you still engaged by the
dark lady of the sonnets in New York? I do hope you will
come to New Orleans with her, and if Sylvia—yes, that
is her name—is still down here—she threatens to get a job
here—something very interesting might develop for you . . .

I hope that this new girl will continue to give you
interest if not happiness in New York. Or Vermont.

Ever,
Tenn.

P.S. I am so shy with this girl Sylvia that I suffer acutely
when alone in a room with her. Have you ever felt that
way with anyone? I have told her I feel that way—she
makes it worse by enquiring every few minutes, 'Am I
making you uncomfortable, do you want me to go out
now? Is it all right if I sit here? Don't talk to me unless
you want to, Etc.' Then she sits there with her brilliant
smile taking in every embarrassed change of expression
as if she were conducting some marvelous experiment
in a lab so that I don't know where to look let alone what
to say. Exactly like Lillian Gish or at best Harold Lloyd
in an old silent film. What are women made of?

WHEELWRIGHT, JACK

THE ECCENTRIC BOSTON POET

I began to take Wheels seriously when I heard of the event at the house of Miss Mason. I shall call him Wheels for that is how he referred to himself; but his name was John Brooks Wheelwright. He came of a New England family so old that an ancestress had been carried off by the Indians, though she was released unharmed. She probably frightened her captors; great determination ran in the Wheelwright blood. Miss Mason, a rich Boston spinster, had a large house on Commonwealth Avenue near Dartmouth Street. (It has been torn down now for a block of apartments.)

That evening Miss Mason was giving one of her elaborate soirées in the ballroom of her home. There was music from a string quartet. Two footmen were serving apple juice; Miss Mason did not approve of champagne. The company were dressed in full regalia and so was Wheels when he was announced and entered the room. Tails and white tie. Surveying the scene with his head slightly cocked and his aristocratic nose a bit in the air, he stood for a few moments by the double door which was flanked by dwarf palm trees in tubs. No one seemed to have noticed his entrance. That would never do.

Kneeling, he lifted the Aubusson, inserted his lanky person beneath it and crawled clear across the whole long room to his cousin's chair. Shocked silence—what would be his next eccentric escapade?—and then laughter and applause as he completed his travel and knelt at Miss Mason's feet. He puffed a bit, a mole coming up for air. Despite his politics, he was somewhere halfway between a Socialist and a Christian Anarchist, Wheels was beloved in Boston society.

He died walking home one night whilst tipsy, was struck & killed by a car where Marlborough (his street) crosses Mass Ave.

WRITING

This vernal season finds me camped with Rexroth on Potrero
Hill, turning out mighty mounds daily of long overdue correspondence, handling through gamuts of gooz masquerading as
manuscripts, translating Part II of *Faust* with MacIntyre, and
pondering astrological movements. The people next door keep
a cock on their upstairs porch and he salutes the dawn very
punctually at four. This is a most mortal sound, which reminds
a man that though love and art be long the old gut is gamboling
fast toward the gravybox and he had better hurry to set down in
immortal fiction his record of his time.

WILSON, EDMUND

F. Scott Fitzgerald's *The Crack-Up* went through about five
printings, and we keep it in print. But I got me in Dutch with
Edmund Wilson because the papers came from him and I did-
n't show him proofs until it was too late. He had systematically crossed out the name of every friend they'd had at
Princeton, though the book said nothing bad about them. And
I put the names back in, John Peale Bishop and this one and
that one. Edmund wrote to me on one of his cards, "You are an
impudent puppy."

WILLIAM CARLOS WILLIAMS

Such a dear man. There was a kind of innocence. What to do about the satyriasis? Maybe do that by recounting the story of the *Dream of Love*, where he imagines he has a heart attack in some doll's shower. I'm very selective. But Bill went for anything that moved. Poor Floss, she got very fed up with it. I must tell about how he loved flowers—the little garden back of the kitchen door and over 100 flower poems in the books.

And here is a scene that I don't think Prof. Vendler wd let us put in the film, that Bill told me one day when we had had a few, he had met the novelist Evelyn Scott at a party in the Village, and she called him on the telephone and talked so hot that he got a hard on which lasted, without diminution, all the way across the Geo Washington Bridge till he got to her apt. Now there was a man.

WARHOL, ANDREW

While waiting to see the art director, Warhol would flirt with the secretaries, making them little origami animals. He told one as he was leaving, "I like you, you're so hirsute."

3 more novels of

Ronald Firbank

caprice

vainglory

inclinations

3 more novels of Ronald Firbank

X
Y
Z

XAVIER

As you can see, I'm having my problems with poor old Xavier. All the boys in the office say I shouldn't do it, but I gave him another 5o. Please save this.

From,

George Xavier,
Driver.

To,

Respected Sir,

With all due respects I beg to bring the following few lines for your kind and favourable orders.

While thanking you of helping me with an advance of Ks.50/- a week ago, I am very sorry to trouble you for further advance of Ks.100/- as my wife was admitted into the Suffering Hospital, Rangoon for confinement, and she requires some other treatment and for to such meet the bill I require to the money today. More over if I borrow outside, I had to pay a heavy interest and I am not in a position to/such interest. As a matter of fact there is no one than to approach your goodself. This amount I shall pay Ks.50/- by monthly instalment.

That in the cirucmstances stated above, I pray that my humble request will meet with your approval. Hoping to be favoured with my esteemed request.

Thanking you in anticipation.

Rangoon,   I beg to remain,
                                          Respected Sir,
Dated the 11th March 1967.   Your most obedient servant,

XT

Yours for Xt, through Mary with a smile,
as the Abbot of Gethsemani used to conclude,

Jas

YOUTH

Those serial numbers. Is that the New Math? I never could even understand the old math. At Choate, to keep being top boy when we got to geometry I had to cheat. Fat old Mr. Doughtery, who liked to rub his balls on the corner of his desk, always put the test papers in his desk drawer until he got around to correcting them. I would sneak back to correct my mistakes when the room was empty. I had to be top boy. And I was and never felt guilty. Morals are relative.

But Choate was full of evil. Pinkham, the head of the student council, paid me 25¢ a day to construe his Virgil for him. (In the poem "Among the Roses," he was the one who claimed that he sent up $50 bills and a rose to chorus girls. Maybe he did.) One year at the spring dance he took his girl down into the room under the chapel and humped her on the leather sofa where the Head used to meditate before giving his sermons. I know because he bet Barkhausen and me he was going to do it and we watched through the little window. Pinkham became head of a big advertising agency in New York. It was my Latin that did it.

YOUTH

*Count Albertu di Marmosa, the duke of Rocamosa, Prince
Faussigny Lucinge, Countess Rünerskeich, Princess Natasha
Paley, Baron Engel, Baron von den Branden . . . God I wish I
were clean inside like Jim St. John and could shun this glitter
and glamour that is not true and stay with my typewriter and
the green mountains.*

*I don't want there to be any wars at all, and I want to love a
woman with my mind too. I want to be more ashamed than I am
that I am so stupid and such a fool, and I want to change this.
I want to speak German well and read music. I want everyone
to read your poetry and give you money because it makes them
feel good. I want to go to bed.*

YOUTH

I'm plugging away now on the Harvard segment of *Byways*. It
goes slowly as there's so much shame attached to the recollections of my behavior in those days. I'm resolved to limit myself
to one doll baby for each college year; otherwise, it would sound
like an ambulatory brothel.

ZUKOFSKY, LOUIS

I was impressed by Louis Zukofsky, who stayed for two weeks [at
Rapallo]. What an intense mind! But he was not at all impressed
with me. We had little conversation. I simply listened to him
talking to Pound. I think he thought I was a parasite . . .

Nevertheless, Zuk gave me for *ND 1936* the magnificent
"Mantis" sequence, which opens with an intricate sestina. It
was a trial-horse for his long poem "A." (One finds lines from
"Mantis" picked up later.) Then for *ND 1938* he gave me the
whole of the eighth section of "A," all fifty-six pages of it. By
then the great poem was really rolling in all its power and splen-
dor of language, Zuk asked me to describe it in the notes as "an
epic of class struggle." . . . He was an ardent Communist, though
I think he dropped away from the Party after the Moscow trials.
It should be noted that "fascist" Pound, who was already an
admirer of Il Duce, paid no attention to Zukofsky's politics. He
liked his minds and his poetry . . . Zuk was eager to have New
Directions become the regular publisher of his books, I wish we
had, but a small publisher can't do everything. And I realized
that he might be difficult and demanding. So there was a cool-
ing of what had never been exactly warm.

End in Funny Farm.

INDEX

ACKNOWLEDGMENTS:

Grateful acknowledgment is made to Hayden Carruth for permission to reprint his letter to James Laughlin on p. 53: copyright © 2006 by Hayden Carruth; to the Estate of Guy Davenport for permission to reprint his letter to James Laughlin on p. 19: copyright © 2006 by the Estate of Guy Davenport; to the Ernest Hemingway Foundation for permission to reprint Ernest Hemingway's letter to James Laughlin on p. 127: copyright © 2006 The Correspondence of Ernest Hemingway; to the Estate of Jack Kerouac for permission to reprint his letter to James Laughlin on p. 154: copyright © 2006 by the Estate of Jack Kerouac; to the Thomas Merton Legacy Trust for permission to reprint his letter to James Laughlin on p. 187: copyright © 2006 by the Thomas Merton Legacy Trust; to *The Paris Review* for the excerpt from "Guy Davenport: The Art of Fiction No. 174," reprinted courtesy of *The Paris Review* and by permission of the Wylie Agency; to New Directions Publishing Corporation for the excerpt from the letter from Henry Miller to Lawrence Durrell and the excerpt from the letter of Lawrence Durrell to Henry Miller (both on p. 174), which appeared in *The Durrell-Miller Letters, 1935-1980*, Edited by Ian S. MacNiven: copyright © 1962, 1963 by Lawrence Durrell and Henry Miller; to The University of the South and its agent Georges Borchardt for permission to reprint the cables from Tennessee Williams to Maria Britneva (p. 184-185): copyright © 2006 by The University of the South, and to reprint the tribute to James Laughlin read at the National Arts Club (p. 313), which originally appeared in *Tom: The Unknown Tennessee Williams* by Lyle Leverich (W. W. Norton & Company): copyright © 1995 by The University of the South; and to New Directions Publishing Corporation to reprint the letter from Tennessee Williams to James Laughlin (p. 324-325) which appears in *The Selected Letters of Tennessee Williams, Volume II: 1945-1957*, edited by Albert J. Devlin, co-edited by Nancy Tischler: copyright © 2004 by the University of the South; and to W. W. Norton & Company for the two excerpts from William Carlos Williams' letters to James Laughlin (on p. 320-321), which appeared in *William Carlos Williams and James Laughlin: Selected Letters*, edited by Hugh Witemeyer: copyright © 1989 by James Laughlin, copyright © 1989 by the Estate of William Carlos Williams; and to New Directions Publishing Corporation to reprint the excerpts from William Carlos Williams's letters which appeared in *Remembering William Carlos Williams* by James Laughlin: copyright © 1995 by William Eric Williams and Paul H. Williams.

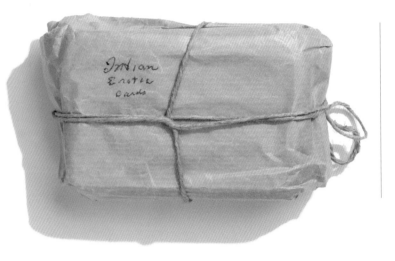

SPECIAL THANKS:
Tom Bean, Susan Chin, Felipe Cruz,
Peter Glassgold, Timothy Hsu,
Leila Laughlin Javitch, Thomas Keith,
Ian MacNiven, Jason Ramirez, Ira Silverberg,
Claudia Steinberg, and The Private
Literary Projects Trust: Trustees,
Peggy L. Fox, Daniel Javitch,
Donald S. Lamm, and
Griselda J. Ohannessian.